A READER'S GUIDE TO
Caspian

A Journey into C. S. Lewis's Narnia

LELAND RYKEN
& MARJORIE LAMP MEAD

IVP Books

An imprint of InterVarsity Press
Downers Grove, Illinois

InterVarsity Press
P.O. Box 1400, Downers Grove, IL 60515-1426
World Wide Web: www.ivpress.com
E-mail: email@ivpress.com

InterVarsity Press® is the book-publishing division of InterVarsity Christian Fellowship/USA®, a student movement active on campus at hundreds of universities, colleges and schools of nursing in the United States of America, and a member movement of the International Fellowship of Evangelical Students. For information about local and regional activities, write Public Relations Dept., InterVarsity Christian Fellowship/USA, 6400 Schroeder Rd., P.O. Box 7895, Madison, WI 53707-7895, or visit the IVCF website at <www.intervarsity.org>.

Design: Rebecca Larson
Images: crown: Gary Godby/iStockphoto
  lion fountain: Eileen Hart/iStockphoto
  Narnia map: drawn by Greg Deddo

ISBN 978-0-8308-3499-0

Printed in the United States of America ∞

Library of Congress Cataloging-in-Publication Data

Ryken, Leland.
  A reader's guide to Caspian: exploring C. S. Lewis's classic story/
Leland Ryken and Marjorie Lamp Mead.
    p. cm.
  Includes bibliographical references and index.
  ISBN-13: 978-0-8308-3499-0 (pbk.: alk. paper)
  1. Lewis, C. S. (Clive Staples), 1898-1963. Prince Caspian. 2.
Children's stories, English—History and criticism. 3. Christian
fiction, English—History and criticism. 4. Fantasy fiction,
English—History and criticism. 5. Narnia (Imaginary place) 6.
Christianity in literature. I. Mead, Marjorie Lamp. II. Title.
  PR6023.E926P7636 2008
  823'.912—dc22

                                                    2007038410

P	19	18	17	16	15	14	13	12	11	10	9	8	7	6	5	4	3	2
Y	24	23	22	21	20	19	18	17	16	15	14	13	12	11	10	09	08

For Jacob and Seth, true Narnians

and

For Dawn Schut Johnson

Contents

PART 2: *CASPIAN* BACKGROUNDS

Preface

Before you begin this book, we would like to make a few suggestions on getting the most out of it. The first is: if you haven't already read *Prince Caspian* in its entirety at least once, or if it has been many years since you last read it, please do so before you go on to part one, "A Guided Tour of *Prince Caspian*." This guide is intended to accompany you on subsequent readings of the book, not to flavor your initial, very personal experience of the story. We cannot overemphasize the importance of this. Your own appreciation will be greatly enhanced if upon your first reading you simply allow this wonderful story to unfold before you. Lewis himself would recommend this approach.

J. R. R. Tolkien understood well the importance of meeting a story directly, upon the first reading, without filtering it through the words of another. In an unfinished introduction to George MacDonald's fairy tale *The Golden Key,* Tolkien advised:

> DON'T READ THIS! Not yet. This is a famous fairy tale. I hope you will like it. That is all that needs to be said, as an "introduction." . . . The author meant to speak direct to his reader, and did not want any one else to interfere, telling the reader to notice this or that, or to understand that or this, before the tale had even begun. . . . So do not pay any attention to me. At any rate until you have read the tale. For what is wrong with "introductions" is their place. They should come second . . . and be like the talks a reader might have with other people who have read the tale; they might lead to sharing of pleasure, or to debate on disagreements; and so lead even to a second reading. . . .

And after the reading . . . there might be questions that you would like to ask. . . . It might be interesting then to hear what some one else has to say, some one who perhaps knew the [author], or his books better or for a longer while. If [you find that the story] is interesting and if you want to hear more, then read this.

And so it is in the spirit of Tolkien's advice that we say to those who are about to embark upon our reader's guide to *Prince Caspian:* "DON'T READ THIS! Not yet." Instead, curl up in a corner somewhere quiet and settle down to read C. S. Lewis's delightful story of *Prince Caspian* on your own. And once you have enjoyed this classic tale in its superb and unique richness, then pick up this reader's guide once again and join with us in conversation about story generally and the tale of *Prince Caspian* in particular.

This guidebook has two basic purposes—to introduce C. S. Lewis's *Prince Caspian* and to give readers some assistance in the basic principles of reading literature. After our earlier volume on *The Lion, the Witch and the Wardrobe* was published (*A Reader's Guide Through the Wardrobe,* InterVarsity Press, 2005), we found that many of our readers responded as appreciatively to the general helps on the reading of story as they did to our specific focus on Lewis's Narnian tale. We hope that will be true for this volume as well.

It may also be helpful to note that this book is intended for adult readers (high school age and above) of this classic children's story, though advanced readers of a younger age will find much to interest them here as well. We encourage parents to make use of this guide as they read *Prince Caspian* with their children. Our background information on the story, as well as our reflection questions, will aid you as you share in this rich reading experience together. We might add that *Prince Caspian* is an excellent read-aloud book, if you are so inclined. In the same way, teachers for all age groups will find the resource material to be of assistance as they discuss the story with their students. And finally we have prepared specific

suggestions to assist both home schoolers and book group discussion leaders (see appendices B and C).

And so we begin. We look forward to your company on this literary
journey.

Introduction

The role of a reader's guide is similar to that of a tour leader. Its primary purpose is to set an itinerary of places to be visited and also to point out details as the successive sites are encountered. In order to do this most effectively, a good tour leader provides a preliminary packet of information. This introduction is our preliminary packet of information for our fellow travelers. It alerts you to the specifics you will most benefit from knowing before you start your literary journey through C. S. Lewis's *Prince Caspian*.

COMPOSITION AND PUBLICATION

When C. S. Lewis began writing *The Lion, the Witch and the Wardrobe,* he had no intention of composing additional Narnian tales. But even before he had finished this first volume, he had already begun to get ideas for another story—a "prequel" that was to precede *The Lion, the Witch and the Wardrobe* chronologically and that would describe how Narnia came into existence. This initial attempt by Lewis to explain the origins of his imaginary world was not successful, but his incomplete twenty-six-page manuscript still survives and is known as *The Lefay Fragment* (see boxed note). Some elements of this early draft eventually made their way into other Narnian books, but of particular note to this guide is the presence of the character Pattertwig (a friendly red squirrel who ended up becoming a part of the story of *Prince Caspian*).

Putting this false start aside for the moment, Lewis altered course and began work on a sequel instead. Brief comments that Lewis jotted down in a notebook give us some idea of possible story lines he was at one time considering. The first two plot concepts bear distinct similarity to (as well

The Lefay Fragment

This unfinished Narnian story most strongly anticipates elements of what eventually became The Magician's Nephew. *In particular, in this fragment we are introduced to Digory, an orphan who lives in a house in London with his difficult Aunt Gertrude. As the story unfolds, we meet Digory's wise godmother, Mrs. Lefay, as well as Polly, the girl next door. The most striking difference between this fragment and* The Magician's Nephew *is Digory's ability to understand the language of the Trees and the Animals (such as the squirrel Pattertwig) while still in England. When Lewis returned to work on this story years later, he did not give Digory these same powers during his London days but rather confined his ability to speak with Talking Beasts to his sojourn in the land of Narnia. Those who are interested in knowing more about this early Narnian manuscript can read the published version in Walter Hooper's* Past Watchful Dragons. *The original of this manuscript fragment is housed at the Bodleian Library, Oxford.*

as differences from) another Narnian tale, *The Voyage of the "Dawn Treader,"* but it is the final notation on this list that points us toward the narrative that eventually became *Prince Caspian*. Lewis's notes read as follows: "SEQUEL TO L.W.W. The present tyrants to be Men. Intervening history of Narnia told nominally by the Dwarf but really an abstract of his story which amounts to telling it in my own person." Those who are acquainted with *Prince Caspian* will recognize the strong parallels between this description and the unfolding of Narnian history as taught by Dr. Cornelius to his young pupil, Caspian. (In this retelling of Narnian history, however, there are layers within layers, as the overall story of Caspian and Cornelius is actually conveyed by another dwarf, Trumpkin, directly to the Pevensie children.)

A comment by Lewis in a letter of September 17, 1949, to an American, Vera Mathews, gives us an indication of when he most likely began working on this new story line in earnest: "A good idea for a (children's) story which also arrived this morning, I suppose from the subconscious, bode well for a good day." In any case, we do know that Lewis wrote *Prince Caspian* sometime during the autumn of that year, as it was in final manuscript form before the end of December 1949. Indeed, once Lewis began the actual writing of his Narnian sequel, its composition flowed swiftly upon the heels of *The Lion, the Witch and the Wardrobe.* Lewis completed *The Lion, the Witch and the Wardrobe* sometime between the end of March and May 1949, while *Prince Caspian* was written, revised and put into final typescript by February 1950—less than one year later. The other Narnian tales followed in rapid succession. In fact, Lewis threw himself into the venture with such energy that he completed the first five Narnian books in a span of less than three years (between the summer of 1948 and the early spring of 1951).

The actual publication sequence of the stories flowed smoothly as well. The first Narnian book to be written, *The Lion, the Witch and the Wardrobe,* was published in autumn 1950, while the second one, *Prince Caspian,* was published in October 1951, issued simultaneously by Geoffrey Bles in England and Macmillan in the United States. Each of the

Roger Lancelyn Green and
the Manuscript of Prince Caspian

We can roughly date the completion of Prince Caspian *to December 1949 because we know Lewis sent the finished manuscript to his friend and former pupil Roger Lancelyn Green, to ask for his comments on the story. Green returned the manuscript to Lewis, along with his suggested revisions, at a luncheon gathering at Magdalen College on December 31—the occasion when Lewis first met Pauline Baynes, the chosen illustrator for* The Lion, the Witch and the Wardrobe. *In addition to helping with* Prince Caspian, *Green gave Lewis encouragement and editorial suggestions as he wrote each one of his Narnian stories.*

other five Narnian volumes followed one per year thereafter, culminating with the seventh story in the series, *The Last Battle,* which was published in 1956.

Publication History of Prince Caspian

1939	*Lewis makes his first tentative attempts to write a children's story (Aslan is not a character in this tale).*
August 1948	*American scholar Chad Walsh learns Lewis is writing a story in the "tradition of E. Nesbit."*
March–May 1949	The Lion, the Witch and the Wardrobe *is finished.*
June 1949	*Lewis is working on a new story that will explain the origins of Narnia; his initial efforts prove unsuccessful and he sets it aside.*
September 1949	*Lewis begins work on a sequel to* The Lion, the Witch and the Wardrobe.
December 1949	*The first draft of the sequel (Lewis's second Narnian story, which will eventually be titled* Prince Caspian*) is complete.*
December 31, 1949	*Lewis meets Pauline Baynes, his chosen illustrator for* The Lion, the Witch and the Wardrobe *(and eventually the other six Narnian tales as well).*
February 1950	Prince Caspian *(under the early title of* A Horn in Narnia*) is in typescript.*
June 22, 1950	*Proofs of* The Lion, the Witch and the Wardrobe *are being read.*
October 16, 1950	The Lion, the Witch and the Wardrobe *is published in hardback by Geoffrey Bles (London).*
November 7, 1950	The Lion, the Witch and the Wardrobe *is published in hardback by Macmillan (New York).*
October 1951	Prince Caspian *is published in hardback in London by Geoffrey Bles and in New York by Macmillan.*

THE PLACE OF *PRINCE CASPIAN* WITHIN THE NARNIAN SERIES

As we have already noted, *Prince Caspian* was composed as the second book in the Narnian series, following *The Lion, the Witch and the Wardrobe*. This is what scholars term the order of composition, and in this instance it is also the publication order of the books. But if we piece together the overall narrative of the seven Narnian books as a group (the so-called chronological order, as distinct from the composition and publication order), *Prince Caspian* is fourth, following *The Magician's Nephew* (first), *The Lion, the Witch and the Wardrobe* (second) and *The Horse and His Boy* (third). For the reasons we think the books are best experienced in the order of composition and publication, see the appendix of our book *A Reader's Guide Through the Wardrobe: Exploring C. S. Lewis's Classic Story* (InterVarsity Press, 2005). In brief, we recommend that you read *The Lion, the Witch and the Wardrobe* first, so that you are able to come to the story with the same sense of the unknown that Lucy and her three siblings bring to their initial visit to the land of Narnia. Only in this way will you be able to imaginatively experience the mystery of who Aslan is (since his identity is only gradually made known to both the children and the reader). In fact, reading any of the other Narnian stories before *The Lion, the Witch and the Wardrobe* means that the reader loses the opportunity to fully experience this literary suspense—an unfolding sense of wonder that Lewis carefully creates in his first tale.

THE TITLE IS CHOSEN

The book's current title came into existence only after an arduous process of trial and error. Lewis himself first proposed the title *Drawn into Narnia*, a designation that underscores the motif of the magical summons around which the story is built. The publisher, Geoffrey Bles, turned down that title as being too difficult to pronounce. Lewis's next suggestion, *A Horn into Narnia*, also highlighted the book's enchanted summons (by referencing Susan's magic horn, which calls the children back into Narnia), but this title was likewise rejected by his publisher.

The eventual solution to the dilemma resulted in a subtitle of which many readers are unaware: *The Return to Narnia*. This volume is the only one of Lewis's Narnian stories to have a subtitle, and it came about as a result of Lewis's dissatisfaction with the main title. As his biographer and friend George Sayer later recalled, "The title [finally] adopted, *Prince Caspian*, was suggested by his publisher. [Lewis] was reluctant to accept it, as it did not in any way suggest the theme of the book. But he had to be content with a subtitle."

Given the relative obscurity accorded by readers to the book's subtitle, it appears that Lewis was justified in believing that it would not adequately address his concern about the misleading main title. It could certainly be argued that as important as Caspian is to the action of the story, he is nonetheless only one in a cast of numerous significant characters. Further, even the designation of prince does not truly take into account the entire tale, as Caspian is finally crowned the *king* of Narnia by the end of the book. Thus, in terms of the title of this story, we do well to remember that Lewis preferred the emphasis to be upon the fact that the children were drawn back into Narnia—without any decision or action on their part, but simply as a result of the needs of others.

WHAT LEWIS HIMSELF SAID ABOUT *PRINCE CASPIAN*

In various letters to his readers C. S. Lewis sprinkled helpful particulars about how he viewed *Prince Caspian*. Responding on December 24, 1959, to the questions of a schoolgirl, Sophia Storr, Lewis endeavored to explain that he did not intentionally plan the Christian elements of his Narnian tales at the outset. But rather, as the story of Aslan and his sacrificial death and subsequent resurrection unfolded in *The Lion, the Witch and the Wardrobe*, the Christian character of this book became apparent. Thus, once he perceived how his first story was shaping, the "whole series became Christian." However, he also made it clear that he did not intend for any of the Narnian books to be understood as allegory. And specifically, in terms of the Christian story line for *Prince Caspian,* he wrote Sophia that in this volume "the old stories about Him [i.e., Aslan] are beginning to be disbelieved."

A further confirmation of Lewis's eventual design for the entire seven-volume Chronicles of Narnia is found in a letter written to another young correspondent, Anne Waller Jenkins, on March 5, 1961, where he declares that "the whole Narnian story is about Christ." But as in his previous letter, Lewis was careful to describe the Christian framework of his children's stories as being distinct from an allegory (where significant aspects of the story would have a one-to-one correspondence to spiritual realities). To clarify the difference between a traditional allegory and his approach, Lewis explained that he intended his stories to serve as an answer to a hypothetical question: if we suppose that there really were a world like Narnia that had gone wrong (in the same way that Christian theology teaches that our own world has fallen and needs redemption), how might Christ enter into Narnian history in order to save it? Lewis scholars have termed this literary approach as a supposal rather than an allegory, as in "suppose" there were a world like Narnia. In addition to this general explanation, Lewis also went on to give detailed summaries of each of his seven books, wherein he described the story line of *Prince Caspian* as being about the "restoration of the true religion after a corruption."

C. S. Lewis's *comment on the nature of allegory to a young girl:*
"A *strict allegory is like a puzzle with a solution: a great romance [or fantasy or myth]*
is like a flower whose smell reminds you of something you can't quite place.
I *think the something is 'the whole quality of life as we actually experience it.' "*

C. S. LEWIS, *LETTERS TO CHILDREN*

It is also interesting to note that shortly before his death on November 7, 1963, Lewis commented to another correspondent that sales of *Prince Caspian* indicated that it was *"longo intervallo* [by a long interval] the least popular of the Narnian books." Unfortunately a sales breakdown on individual volumes of the Narnian series is not available, so it is not possible to know whether this is still the case. Overall, the seven volumes have sold more than 100 million copies worldwide since they were first published in the 1950s, and not one of the stories has ever been out of print. As a result, even if the sales figures on *Prince Caspian* have continued to lag behind the other six books, there is no doubt that it must still be ranked as one of the most successful children's stories of all time, in terms of total sales.

The Unifying Action of *Prince Caspian*

Lewis's narrative imagination was extraordinarily active in this story. We can infer that Lewis became so exhilarated by the process of inventing scenes and details that he produced a story notable for its wide range of material. Since it would be easy not to see the forest for the trees, it is important to know from the start that in spite of the abundant variety packed into this narrative, the story nonetheless does possess a required unity of action (a literary attribute considered a requirement from the time of Aristotle's *Poetics*).

The unifying action of *Prince Caspian* is the struggle of the forces of good (known in the story as Old Narnia) to regain the land of Narnia from the forces of evil. When the story opens, the current malevolent rulers have become so powerful and pervasive that they have endeavored to stamp out even the memory of Old Narnia (which is also referred to, at times, as Aslan's country). Nearly everything in the narrative contributes to this central plot conflict, which the reader can see to be heading toward a climactic battle between the opposing sides. It is interesting to note that the story line of *Prince Caspian* parallels that of *The Lion, the Witch and the Wardrobe,* which is also unified by the struggle of Aslan and his followers working to wrest control of Narnia from the forces of evil (see boxed note).

In the previous paragraph we noted that "nearly everything" in this tale contributes to the central action. We said that because stories always progress by a back-and-forth rhythm between scenes of heightened tension

Parallels with The Lion, the Witch and the Wardrobe

- The plot structure of the first two Narnian books is similar, being built around the arrival of the four Pevensie children in Narnia and their journey to reach the Stone Table. In the second book the Stone Table has been renamed Aslan's How (or Mound).

- In both stories the land of Narnia is in bondage to an agent of evil (the White Witch and King Miraz, respectively) from whom it needs to be liberated.

- In both stories there is a decisive battle of Aslan's forces against an evil army, with Peter playing a heroic role in the battles.

- In The Lion, the Witch and the Wardrobe Aslan himself is resurrected, and in Prince Caspian Aslan reawakens various forces of nature back to life.

- In The Lion, the Witch and the Wardrobe Aslan transforms the stone statues into their living creaturely forms, and in Prince Caspian he transforms a village and its environs back into the forms they had in Old Narnia.

- In both stories the reclaimed land of Narnia is entrusted at the end of the story to virtuous rulers.

and scenes of relaxation to offset the intensity of the episodes of conflict. Some of the interspersed celebration scenes in *Prince Caspian* are somewhat peripherally attached to the main conflict, even though the same characters appear in both types of episodes.

A SEQUEL TO *THE LION, THE WITCH AND THE WARDROBE*

As we pointed out earlier, *Prince Caspian* is a sequel to the first Narnian book. Virtually all the original reviewers seized upon this connection (see our chapter on contemporary reviews). Of course *Prince Caspian* is not a traditional sequel in that it does not directly continue the action of the first story. Rather, *Prince Caspian* is a sequel in the sense that it contains numerous references to events that happened during the Pevensie siblings' earlier visit to Narnia as told in *The Lion, the Witch and the Wardrobe*. This does not mean that you cannot understand the action of *Prince Caspian* without having read the first book, since storytellers often make enticing references to places and events that we only learn about for the first time as we read a particular story. But it does mean that you will miss many of the deeper meanings of *Prince Caspian* and will sometimes be mystified by certain narrative references if you are not already familiar with *The Lion, the Witch and the Wardrobe*.

AN ADVENTURE STORY

One of the glories of the Narnian stories is the way in which Lewis managed to bring multiple genres together in the books. To observe how these genres converge is one of the pleasures of a sophisticated level of reading the books.

The genre of the adventure story may be the dominant one in *Prince Caspian*. The staples of an adventure story are the following: surface excitement; an aura of the unusual, the extraordinary and the remote, as opposed to the commonplace; use of sensational settings, characters and events as a way of producing that atmosphere; variety of story material (constantly shifting settings and characters and widely divergent types of action); reliance on the motifs of conflict, danger, suspense, horror, surprise and spectacular feats; inclusion of such stock situations as battles, journeys, storms, dangerous landscapes, hiding, arrest, imprisonment and narrow escapes.

A FAIRY TALE

Prince Caspian is also a fairy tale. Fairy tales are a simple and primitive form of literature—folk literature, appealing to simple literary tastes as well as sophisticated literary tastes. Because fairy stories tap our elemental experiences, they present simplified and heightened pictures of good and evil, not subtle intermixtures of them. Mainly, though, we associate fairy stories with certain stock story ingredients: inclusion of supernatural or marvelous settings, characters and events; as part of the supernaturalism, inclusion of what in fairy tales is termed magic; evocation of horror; humanlike animals as characters; a sinister forest; castles; villainous characters such as witches, hags and other monstrous creatures; heroes and heroines; kings, queens, princes and princesses.

FANTASY AND MYTH

The categories of fairy tale, fantasy and myth overlap. Fantasy is perhaps the broadest of these categories and refers to literature that specializes in what literary critics for centuries have called "the marvelous." This means that it includes settings, characters and events that are unlifelike. In other words, there are definite elements in these types of tales that *would* not and *could* not be found in our everyday existence. As a result, fantasy stories are most often set in another world—a fantasy world such as C. S. Lewis's land of Narnia. (Fairy tales are heavily fantastic, but in addition they have the traits listed in the preceding section, and these make fairy tales a realm *within* fantasy.)

Myth is extreme fantasy—literature that goes to the highest possible degree of supernaturalism. Talking animals belong to fantasy and fairy tales, but divine or semidivine beings are mythical. *Prince Caspian* is mainly a fantasy story, but the character of Aslan and many of the creatures that make up Old Narnia are mythical beings. Narnia itself is primarily a fantasyland, but the deep longings that it awakens in us give it the quality of myth as well. Mythic tales present a sense of awe that goes beyond the ordinary natural world and thereby moves us into an awareness of a spiritual realm infused with transcendent realities.

A CHILDREN'S BOOK

The category of children's literature is also relevant to our reading of *Prince Caspian*. Loosely defined, a children's story is a story that contains the narrative elements that children enjoy most. The list of those preferences includes the following things: children as the protagonists of the story; portrayal of children's experiences and a view of the world as children see it;

attentiveness to childhood fears and longings; animals and other nonhuman beings as characters. In particular, *Prince Caspian* has more nonhuman characters than named human characters, a strong indication that it is a children's book.

Lewis also believed that children (as well as many adult readers) especially enjoy stories with descriptive episodes that reflect a sense of what he termed "homeliness." By homeliness he did not mean unattractiveness but rather an atmosphere of domestic comfort that conveys an appreciation for ordinary, everyday pleasures. Most often these scenes supply a needed break from intense action and allow the reader to "recover" before the next adventure begins. An example of this element of homeliness in *Prince Caspian* occurs in chapter six when Caspian is introduced to various Old Narnians and pauses to eat a refreshing noonday meal of oatcakes, apples, herbs, wine and cheese with the Centaurs.

Children as Narnian Critics

The typescript of Prince Caspian *was read to the children of Oxford University law professor F. H. Lawson with "enthusiastic results" before it was ever published. This trial reading occurred in early 1950, months before* The Lion, the Witch and the Wardrobe *was issued that following October. Undoubtedly the approval of the Lawson children was a helpful encouragement to Lewis at this point in the creative process, as previously he had received only adult feedback on his as-yet-unpublished Narnian stories. Though never a close friend, Lawson had been a frequent luncheon companion of Lewis in the late 1920s and early 1930s.*

THE RELIGIOUS DIMENSION OF THE STORY

There is nothing so theologically overt in *Prince Caspian* as the depiction of Aslan's atoning death and resurrection that is to be found in *The Lion, the Witch and the Wardrobe.* Rather, in *Prince Caspian,* the approach to spiritual

experience is more indirect, though the book covers more general theological topics than does *The Lion, the Witch and the Wardrobe.* Nonetheless the
spiritual aspect of *Prince Caspian* is just as significant and moving as was true
of the earlier story.

To fully realize the religious dimension, we need to make an equation of
Aslan with Christ, but that is easy to do in light of the action in *The Lion, the
Witch and the Wardrobe*—as well as Lewis's own statements as noted earlier.
In the middle of *Prince Caspian,* the issue of being able or not able to see
Aslan becomes a leading narrative motif. This is partly a question of faith,
that is, believing in an unseen supernatural realm based on what God (or the
character of Aslan, primarily) has revealed about it. But just as importantly,
seeing and following Aslan (Christ) means obediently relating to him in
daily life. Within this frame of reference, the events in the story remind us
at numerous points of aspects of the Christian life (for example, Lucy's initially unheeded but later acknowledged witness to others about her having
seen and been instructed by Aslan).

In the world of *Prince Caspian* the characters are divided into two basic
categories—those who know and love Aslan and those who either do not acknowledge his existence or else hate him and his rule. This is the basic
Christian paradigm, both in the Bible and the Christian's life in the world.

ℯ～ᵭ

With the preceding elements as our foundational guide, we are now ready
to turn to the story of *Prince Caspian* itself. As a final reminder, if you have
not yet read this Narnian tale in its entirety, it is best to do so now, before
you turn to part one.

PART ONE

A Guided Tour of *Prince Caspian*

The Island

HOW LEWIS DECIDED TO BEGIN HIS STORY

The story line of chapter one: The four Pevensie children are waiting on an English railway platform on their way back to school when a magical summons tugs them unexpectedly out of this world and returns them to the land of Narnia. Unceremoniously plopped into an unfamiliar landscape, they find themselves in the midst of a dense forest, located close by the sea, where their second adventure in Narnia begins.

The biggest test for storytellers comes on the first two pages. That is where they need to capture readers' attention to such a degree that they want to keep reading. Novelist E. M. Forster was of the opinion that a story "can have only one merit: that of making the audience want to know what happens next. And conversely it can only have one fault: that of making the audience not want to know what happens next." We can rest assured that C. S. Lewis gave careful thought as to how to arouse his readers' interest at the beginning of his story, and correspondingly we can enjoy analyzing the devices he seized upon.

The means by which C. S. Lewis captivates us at the beginning of this story are multiple, and exploring them yields a lot. Before we do that, though, it is important to note that on the first two pages Lewis juggles several balls in the air, including the following: (1) he reintroduces us to the four siblings of the Narnian series; (2) he serves notice that the story we are about to read is a sequel to *The Lion, the Witch and the Wardrobe*; (3) he establishes the time as one year after the children's first excursion into Narnia as narrated in the earlier story; (4) he evokes a sense of everyday British realism by situating the children in a train station en route to going their separate ways to different schools.

ℭℯ *For Reflection or Discussion*

Lewis needs to captivate us right at the outset, even before the children are whisked away to Narnia. He does so by time-honored tricks of the literary trade. You might ponder how the following techniques make an appearance in these opening pages:

- a variation of the "once upon a time" formula
- everyday realism, leading us to resonate affectionately with the real-life details that are placed before us (such as four children on a British railway platform waiting for a train). As with any author, Lewis often included favorite specifics in his stories. Those familiar with Lewis's life know that he was fond of traveling by railway.
- evocation of mystery (for example, the references to the children's experience of the passage of many years in Narnia, along with the implication that no time at all had elapsed in the real world of England during the extended period they spent in Narnia)
- the introduction of characters (the four Pevensie children) about whose destinies we are made to care
- the skillful description of details and setting that transports us imaginatively from our own everyday world to the fictional world of the story. Once again, it is interesting to know that as a young boy Lewis reveled in his month-long holidays at the seaside with his mother and brother. Consider how these memories may have informed his description of the island coast and the children's discussion of gathering gulls' eggs or catching shrimp (activities Lewis knew from his own boyhood).

Transition to the Strange World

The first task of a storyteller is to transport us to the world of the story. But in a fantasy story like *Prince Caspian,* an even more important transport occurs—the movement from the known world to the fantastical world of the story. In *Prince Caspian* the transport is more abrupt than in *The Lion, the Witch and the Wardrobe*. Instead of a gradual transition through the back of

Entering Narnia

Here is how C. S. Lewis chose to depict the moments of transition from his fictional "real world" to Narnia in each one of his seven children's stories:

- The Lion, the Witch and the Wardrobe (*1950*). *There are multiple entries into Narnia in this first tale, but each one occurs when one or more of the children (first Lucy alone, then Lucy followed by Edmund, and finally all four Pevensie children together) go through the same entryway—a magical wardrobe that serves, intermittently in the story, as a doorway to Narnia.*

- Prince Caspian (*1951*). *The four children (Peter, Susan, Edmund and Lucy) are "pulled" abruptly back into Narnia when Prince Caspian blows Susan's enchanted Horn in a moment of need.*

- The Voyage of the "Dawn Treader" (*1952*). *Lucy, Edmund and Eustace enter Narnia by way of a painting that comes to life.*

- The Silver Chair (*1953*). *Eustace and Jill ask Aslan for help and then find an unlocked door in the garden wall that leads them into Narnia.*

- The Horse and His Boy (*1954*). *This is the one Narnian story that does not have a transition into Narnia, as the story takes place during the years when the four children (Peter, Susan, Edmund and Lucy) reigned as kings and queens over the inhabitants of Narnia. In other words, the action of this tale occurs during the final few pages of* The Lion, the Witch and the Wardrobe.

- The Magician's Nephew (*1955*). *In this story about the origins of Narnia, a magician uses trickery and magic rings to send two children, Polly and Digory, into other worlds, including Narnia at its creation.*

- The Last Battle (*1956*). *In this final story in the Narnian chronicles, seven friends of Narnia, children from the earlier stories, are thrust suddenly back into Narnia as the result of a train wreck in England.*

a wardrobe into a wintry landscape, the children are pulled instantaneously from a railway platform into the strangeness of an unknown world, as the platform and everything on it simply vanish and the children find themselves in a spooky, overgrown "woody place."

Once the children are out of our world and into this other world, Lewis's task is to establish the nature of the world we have entered with them. We know that Lewis valued atmosphere as a story quality (in connection with the classic tale of *The Three Musketeers* he complained, "The total lack of atmosphere repels me"). Accordingly, Lewis lavishes his first attention on creating the appropriate sense of atmosphere—in this instance, the feeling of being on an island surrounded by water.

It is important to note at the outset of our journey through *Prince Caspian* that this is a story built out of archetypes. Archetypes are the master images of the imagination that recur throughout literature and life itself. They are plot motifs (such as the journey or ordeal), character types (such as the hero or traitor) or images (such as the sinister forest or happy valley). Archetypes evoke primal and universal human feelings and thereby aid the author in telling the story. For example, when a character finds herself walking through a dark and tangled wood, we, as readers, are immediately alerted to the fact that she is in a potentially risky situation. We understand this without the author's directly saying so, because we intuitively recognize the sinister forest motif and its danger-laden implications.

Cⅇ *For Reflection or Discussion*

In the final movement of the opening chapter of *Prince Caspian*, Lewis will move from the general qualities of the place to which the children have been transported to foreshadowings of the fact that the children have actually arrived at their old castle, Cair Paravel. This middle section of the chapter needs to be relished as a triumph of evocative description. One grid through which to mold your impressions is to note the particular qualities of the atmosphere that Lewis builds up through a wealth of particular details. For example, there is present a sense of danger, of seclusion, of lostness and of a struggle for survival (as the hungry children begin to scavenge for food). A second, overlapping analytic grid is to note the archetypes. Just for starters in the opening of this story, we encounter the secluded island, the forlorn coast and the deserted woods.

A SCENE OF DISCOVERY

The more detailed discovery scene of Cair Paravel in ruins will happen in the next chapter, but Lewis prepares us for the unfolding of this surprise in the last page and a half of the opening chapter. After a general survey of the island, which for all its wild qualities has overtones of the archetypal fertile earthly paradise, we zoom in on a specific site. The transition to that site comes with the mention of an apple tree that Lucy discovers. The discovery of this lone apple tree expands into the sighting of dozens of others, leading Susan to identify the place as an orchard (itself an archetype with positive connotations), with Peter thereby deducing that the island on which they have landed was at one time inhabited.

Suddenly our curiosity is aroused. This curiosity becomes intensified as details continue to unfold, especially the discovery of a stone wall with the intriguing architectural detail of a great, though decayed, archway. Lewis does not give us a lengthy description, but the few specifics that he offers are hugely evocative. Storytellers love to end chapters on a note of mystery and with an implied notation "to be continued." The ending of chapter one in *Prince Caspian* is a masterpiece of this anticipatory technique.

> ## ℭ *For Reflection or Discussion*
>
> A good strategy when reading a long story is to pause at the end of every chapter and take stock before moving on to the next chapter. Two questions are especially important: (1) What narrative business has been transacted in this chapter? In other words, how does the chapter fit into the ongoing design of the story? (2) What things stand out most vividly in my impressions as I look back at my experience of reading the chapter?

ℭ 2 ℮

The Ancient Treasure House

A DISCOVERY STORY

The story line of chapter two: After following a stream inland through the thick woods, Peter, Susan, Edmund and Lucy have stumbled upon an overgrown apple orchard and they recognize that they have also discovered the ruins of a castle. They gradually come to realize that these ruins are the remains of Cair Paravel, their former home in Narnia. Later, while exploring their old treasure chamber, they recover their long-ago presents from Father Christmas (with the exception of Susan's enchanted Horn, which is not with the other gifts).

The storehouse of narrative motifs and types of plots from which storytellers can choose is a veritable treasure trove. C. S. Lewis dipped into that treasure chest for a vast number of differing motifs in *Prince Caspian*, including a greater variety than he employed in any of the other Narnian stories. In chapter two of this book, he made use of the classic discovery story motif.

Discovery stories are structured on a simple principle: the characters in the story keep discovering more and more surprising things. Of course, as readers, we discover these things along with the characters in the story, as together we observe the mystery unfolding. Two additional narrative qualities go hand in hand with the new revelations: the motif of surprise is prominent, and the ongoing series of discoveries quickly turns the tale into a suspense story as well.

ℭℯ *For Reflection or Discussion*

Before proceeding to read the commentary that follows, you may wish to go back to the text and review the series of discoveries that the Pevensie children make, along with the surprises and subsequent suspense that accompany the unfolding action.

You might also want to reflect upon the fact that Lewis enjoyed taking walking tours in the English and Irish countryside. While on these walks, he sometimes encountered the ruins of castles. Undoubtedly these memories informed his description of the Pevensie children's discovery of Cair Paravel.

PHASE ONE: HOW THE CHILDREN NEARLY GET THE POINT

This chapter unfolds in three distinct phases. At the outset the children verge on recognition of their surroundings but then get sidetracked into procuring their essential needs for survival. The element of discovery that they initially achieve is an awareness that they have landed not simply in an orchard (end of chapter one) but also in a ruined castle. They gradually make sense of their new environs by remembering that this place is *like* the castle at Cair Paravel. The narrative dynamic at work is dramatic irony: we readers understand (or at least strongly suspect) that this *is* Cair Paravel, but the children remain ignorant.

Lewis prolongs the irony by devoting a lengthy paragraph to an account of the building of a campfire and the eating of a meal. These types of domestic details do not contribute directly to the ongoing action of the story line, but instead they create a certain type of atmosphere, which Lewis described as the element of "homeliness." The homeliness of this scene lends an elemental quality to the event, as we are reminded that the everyday as-

The Name Cair Paravel

The derivation for the first part of the name of Cair Paravel has two potential sources. In a letter to a Belfast friend, Lewis recorded his delight over various words he encountered while reading Geoffrey of Monmouth's History of the Kings of Britain. *Among the terms was "Kaer," which Lewis noted was British for city. Thus, we have the "city" of Paravel as the name of the Pevensies' castle. Perhaps Lewis was also thinking of the Welsh term, Caer—which means either castle or fort—when he crafted this name.*

As for the second part of the castle's name, Martha Sammons in A Guide Through Narnia *offers that " 'Court Paravail' is an inferior or lower court; a 'Paravail' is one in a position below another but who holds another beneath like a tenant. Lewis is thus implying that while the Kings and Queens rule over Narnia, they, in turn, are in submission to Aslan and the Emperor-Over-the-Sea." Paul Ford, in his* Companion to Narnia, *suggests a slightly different interpretation: "Paravail, from the Old French par aval, meaning 'down,' and Latin ad vallen, 'to the valley.' Thus, Cair Paravel is a 'city in the valley,' and takes its name from its castle."*

pects of life are both pleasurable and necessary, even in situations of extremity. There is also an element of contrast: Cair Paravel, which was once a place of splendor and even opulence, has now become a strange and unknown wilderness where the children struggle to meet their basic needs. In this situation Lewis juxtaposes strangeness (the wilderness) and homeliness (eating food around a campfire)—two elements that he particularly enjoyed finding in a story.

PHASE TWO: LEARNING THAT THIS IS CAIR PARAVEL

When Susan goes to fetch water and comes back with a tiny, pure-gold chess knight, a whole new round of discoveries ensues. The thrill of the developing awareness of the children as they realize that they have indeed landed in Cair Paravel is perpetual. An adult reader might speak of evidential proof—details that prove to the children that this is the castle where they once ruled, only now in a ruined state. In spite of the unexplained time discrepancy (they have been absent from Narnia for only a year, but the castle ruins indicate that hundreds of years have passed since they last lived within its walls), they now have indisputable proof that the "impossible" is reality. Such an incongruity serves to underscore that Narnia remains an enchanted land, where the mysterious occurs with regularity.

PHASE THREE: LOOKING BACK AND LOOKING FORWARD AT THE SAME TIME

A new dimension enters the series of discoveries when the children decide to seek out the special gifts that Father Christmas had given them in *The*

Time on Earth Versus Time in Narnia

Readers of the Chronicles of Narnia should be aware that during the span of the seven books 2,555 Narnian years take place, in contrast to the passage of only fifty-two earthly years. Thus, when the story of Prince Caspian opens, though the Pevensie children have experienced only a single year of earthly time since they left Narnia, in the land of Narnia itself 1,303 years have elapsed. As a result, their castle of Cair Paravel has had many centuries to fall into decay since they last lived there. See chapter eleven, "Through the Wardrobe," in C. S. Lewis: A Biography, by Green and Hooper (2002), for a helpful chronology that Lewis himself composed. This outline of Narnian history illustrates clearly how earthly time intersects with Narnian time.

Lion, the Witch and the Wardrobe. Those gifts had originally been presented to them in their first visit to Narnia as a preparation for battle, and they serve as a similar foreshadowing now. Lucy's bottle contains a magical cordial for the healing of battle wounds. Susan's bow is a weapon of warfare. So, too, are Peter's sword and his shield with the great red Lion on it.

> ### ⟳ *For Reflection or Discussion*
> The impressionistic question is always relevant: among the things that the children discover, which ones are your favorites? Additionally, if you have read *The Lion, the Witch and the Wardrobe*, you can take stock of how various details here are the same for you as they are for the children—"like meeting very old friends." You may even want to make a return trip to *The Lion, the Witch and the Wardrobe*. The motif at work here is a literary convention known as *the place revisited;* you might search your memory for past encounters with that branch of literature. Finally you can comb the last two pages of this chapter in *Prince Caspian* for hints of foreboding.

ℭ 3 ℈

The Dwarf

PLOT, SETTING AND CHARACTER
AS A NARRATIVE HARMONY

The story line of chapter three: The four children rescue a captive Dwarf from two soldiers and save him from death by drowning. Using the boat his captors had abandoned, the Dwarf catches fish for their breakfast. After they all have eaten their fill, the Dwarf begins to tell them what is happening in Narnia at the present moment,

introducing them to the story of Prince Caspian and the Old Narnians and their war
with the traitorous Telmarines.

Good stories are a balancing act in which the storyteller keeps the three
main elements of a story—plot, setting and character—in balance, giving
each its due. If one of the three dominates unduly, the story loses something.
There is such an abundance of adventure (plot material) in *Prince Caspian*
that it could easily have run away with the book. But Lewis gives us memorable characters and evocative settings to keep things in balance.

Plot is primary in the sense that it carries the story forward and provides
the framework within which setting and characterization can exist. Aristotle
is definitive on the subject: "Most important of all is the structure of the in-
cidents." That is true, argued Aristotle, because a story "is an imitation, not
of men, but of an action and of life, and life consists in action. . . . Character
comes in as subsidiary to the actions."

A MINIATURE STORY

Every chapter in a well-told story is a miniature story in itself, replete with
the three parts (beginning, middle, end) that Aristotle said characterize a
complete action. Chapter three has its own shapely pattern, unfolding in five
phases: (1) the children's gradual adjustment to being back in Narnia; (2)
the sudden appearance of two menacing soldiers and a captive Dwarf in a
rowboat; (3) the rescue of the Dwarf; (4) the enjoyment of eating a substantial meal after being hungry; and (5) following the meal, the Dwarf's intriguing mentions of Prince Caspian and the Old Narnians. This last section illustrates once again how storytellers love to end a chapter by propelling us
into the next chapter—in this case, where the Dwarf will continue his story
and explain his references to Old Narnia and Prince Caspian.

The title of chapter three ("The Dwarf") also alerts us as readers to the
fact that there is more to the story than the external action. In the process

of reading, plot absorbs our attention, and in a sense it takes care of itself. It requires a more conscious and reflective effort to mold our impressions of characters into a composite and growing portrait, and then into an understanding of what the storyteller is saying about life by means of these characters. Although our sections in this book labeled "For Reflection or Discussion" do not always include a prompt to analyze the characters, such analysis is continually appropriate, and it will raise your experience of *Prince Caspian* to a more perceptive level to engage in such analysis. It is the mark of good storytellers that they give us depth of characterization in addition to exciting action. Lewis never lets us down in this regard, but we are the ones who need to move beyond the level of the plot to reflection upon the characters.

Applying this to chapter three, once Trumpkin lands on the island and starts to interact with his rescuers, it is possible for us to get to know him.

Mary Clare Havard

C. S. Lewis dedicated Prince Caspian *to the fourteen-year-old daughter of his good friend and personal physician, Robert Havard. Dr. Havard was also a well-liked member of Lewis's literary circle of friends, the Inklings. The doctor in Perelandra—the middle volume of Lewis's space trilogy—was named Humphrey (one of Havard's many affectionate nicknames bestowed upon him by the Inklings) in tribute to this friend.*

His function in this chapter is to serve as our first messenger from the world of Narnia as it exists in this story. He serves as Lewis's internal narrator for a third of the story. But beyond his role as a storyteller, we get to know him personally in this chapter. He is loyal to Old Narnia and therefore represents a moral norm to emulate. He is a take-charge person with mastery of the tasks of daily survival—"a most capable person," the storyteller correctly asserts. He is also a good teller of tales, like the hero of Homer's *Odyssey* when he recounts his wanderings to his hosts in Phaiacia.

As for setting, the third element of stories, it is unlikely to receive a lot of space within the story. What matters, though, is that (a) a sense of setting is kept in our awareness as we progress through a given chapter, and (b) these atmospheric elements are described in vivid and evocative terms when the storyteller does turn to a description of setting. In the chapter under consideration, scattered references to water, boat, fish, apple, creek, castle and fire all help to build up the setting in our imagination—and in so doing they are the crucial attributes that bring the story to life.

◌ *For Reflection or Discussion*

After reading this chapter, here are four good points to go back and explore:

- the attention that Lewis (and he is only doing what other writers of fantasy and adventure stories do) devotes to eating and providing for the sustenance of physical life. In this regard, remember that Lewis especially valued the element of *homeliness* in a story (i.e., the ordinary, everyday aspects of commonplace life). Why do you think he appreciated homeliness so highly? How does its presence serve to heighten our awareness of the *strangeness* of a fantasy world?
- the expanding portrait of Trumpkin the Dwarf, noting the details that make him already come alive in our imagination
- hints that signal the larger story as yet unknown to us and the Pevensie children: about the tyranny of Caspian's uncle that has pushed Old Narnia—the idealized Narnia that existed when the children were last here—into hiding and bondage
- pieces of descriptive data that fall into the category of setting (it yields a lot of analytic mileage to peruse a passage looking for just one thing at a time)

ℭ 4 ♋

The Dwarf Tells of Prince Caspian

THE DEVICE OF FLASHBACK

The story line of chapter four: This chapter recounts the early years of Prince Caspian at the court of his uncle, King Miraz. Caspian's happiest moments as a young child are spent listening to the stories of Old Narnia that his Nurse tells him at bedtime. When Miraz learns of this, however, he is furious. He sends the Nurse away and Caspian receives a Tutor instead—the diminutive Doctor Cornelius. To Caspian's delight, his Tutor proves to be not only a kind and wise teacher but also a half-dwarf who is able to tell his eager pupil the true history of Narnia. But because of Miraz's desire to suppress all memory of Old Narnia, Caspian can learn such things only during secret nighttime conversations held with Doctor Cornelius at the top of the castle's tallest tower.

As the Dwarf begins to tell the children (and us) the story of Prince Caspian's childhood, we might suddenly realize that Lewis has used a technique that we associate particularly with epics. It is known by the Latin phrase *in medias res,* meaning "in the middle of things." On a first reading we might well have concluded that we were reliving the action from the beginning. Now we learn that we were plunged into the story at its midpoint. Chapter four takes us back to earlier action, a technique known as *flashback,* and it exists on multiple levels in this chapter.

THE CAST OF CHARACTERS

We can read the chapter first at the level of characterization. The protagonist of the account is Prince Caspian, and we need to sketch an emerging portrait of the significant things we learn about him, starting here and continuing throughout the book. The overall pattern is familiar in literature and is known as *the growth of the hero*. Ordinarily such a story traces the development of the hero (in this case a king) from childhood to adulthood (and sometimes to death). In many ways Prince Caspian is not as approachable or as friendly a figure to our sensibilities as the other main characters in the story are, but that is appropriate: he is the prince and future king—not just a private citizen but a leader.

Next in prominence is King Miraz, the archetypal usurper of a throne, a tyrant and a villain.

Third in importance is Doctor Cornelius, who fills several roles. Physically he is half dwarf and half human, and the importance of this is that he is Caspian's (and our) bridge between present-day Narnia, which is captive to evil, and Old Narnia, which is the kingdom of Aslan and the archetypal good place. Doctor Cornelius is brought into Caspian's life to be a tutor, and the most important knowledge he conveys is the past history of Narnia. He is thus the imparter of revelation, and as instructor he also has overtones of the sage or wise man. The occurrences that highlight these roles are the

The Name Caspian

Like many authors, C. S. Lewis often made use of imaginative elements from his earlier creative efforts. The name he gave to the character of Prince Caspian is just one of those uses. In an unfinished narrative poem that Lewis wrote when he was twenty-five years old, one of the characters—the older half sister of a boy named Jardis—is named Caspian. Though this character bears no resemblance to the Narnian Caspian and has only a minor mention in this early poem, which is a retelling of the story of Cupid and Psyche, it appears likely that Lewis's initial attraction to the name resurfaced decades later when he was composing Prince Caspian. *As to the original source for the name, Lewis may have encountered it first in a geography lesson: the Caspian Sea is the name for the world's largest landlocked body of water—which is salty, not fresh, and located between Russia and Iran.*

secret trips on which the Doctor leads Caspian to the top of the Great Tower, a point of high elevation from which vision is possible.

Cℯ *For Reflection or Discussion*

You can scrutinize the chapter for details that fill out the characterization of three characters—the youthful Prince Caspian, the tyrannical King Miraz in his prime and the aged Doctor Cornelius. Then there is an outer ring of briefly mentioned characters who are also important, including Caspian's unfortunate Nurse who is deported, the Telmarines as a group and briefly mentioned animals and Dwarfs who belong to Old Narnia.

THE THEME OF THE TWO WORLDS

Characterization is one of two main ingredients in chapter four. The other main item of narrative business is that we are introduced to the theme of the two distinct worlds that serves as the frame of reference for the entire story. It is the clash between Old Narnia and present-day Narnia, which is at the same time also a conflict between good and evil. We should note in passing that our glimpses into the Narnia of the distant past represent a second layer of flashback in this chapter.

As the story unfolds, we intuitively start to compile a list of things that characterize the two distinct realms of Old Narnia and present-day Narnia. Both realms exist in the same geographical place, but they are separated by time. Additionally the two realms are dominated by vastly different values.

The clash between Old Narnia and present-day Narnia exists on two levels. One of these is the level of plot, which is a conflict story that will expand finally to epic magnitude as the book unfolds. The strategy of storytellers is to make us feel more and more uncomfortable and increasingly threatened by the forces of evil before the good triumphs in the end. This chapter gives us plenty of things about which to feel endangered.

But a level of spiritual reality also enters the story in this chapter. Old Narnia was "the country of Aslan" and as such the realm of spiritual goodness. It remains a spiritual norm against which to measure the evils of the present. Suddenly the story takes on overtones of a holy war between God's followers and their adversaries, as in the Old Testament and the book of Revelation. It is no wonder that the young Caspian wants "to go on talking about these things [the story of Old Narnia] for hours and hours and hours."

The story of Narnia about which we hear in this chapter is a degeneration plot in which a country and its citizens deteriorated from good to bad over a period of generations. It is important to note that the worst corruption came from within individuals, and at this point biblical stories about human sinfulness and its destructive effects become a relevant context.

ℭℯ *For Reflection or Discussion*

At least three avenues exist toward reaching an understanding of the juxtaposition of worlds in this chapter:

- At the level of plot conflict, it is important to collect the pieces of data that we receive about how bad things have become in Narnia, with growing discomfort as the evil piles up.
- As we engage in bridge building between Narnia and our own world, including contemporary events, we can see in the practices that prevail in present-day Narnia parallels to dictatorial states as we have known them in our world.
- Then we can explore the conflict between the Telmarines and the values of Old Narnia that can be seen as the age-old spiritual battle between good and evil, between God and his adversaries.

ℰ 5 ℑ

Caspian's Adventure in the Mountains

ESCAPE AND RESCUE

The story line of chapter five: When the previously childless King Miraz has a son and heir, Caspian's life is in danger, so his Tutor helps him to escape, presenting him with Queen Susan's "lost" Horn as a parting gift. After a long night and day of riding, Caspian finds himself in a dark, storm-tossed wood. He is thrown from his horse and awakens in a cave with surprising rescuers: Trufflehunter, a talking Badger, and two Dwarfs—unfriendly Nikabrik and good-natured Trumpkin. To his delighted astonishment, Caspian realizes that he has stumbled across a remnant of Old Narnia.

The action in this chapter falls into a neat three-part sequence: (1) the crisis that requires Caspian to flee for his life; (2) the perilous nighttime journey of escape; and (3) the rescue of Caspian by the Badger Trufflehunter. The dynamics of plot dominate the chapter, and in turn we can organize our experience of the action around several archetypes.

The opening scenario belongs to an esteemed branch of ancient writing and social custom known as *the education of the prince*. The introductory paragraph is the false calm before the storm, as we read about Caspian's pleasant school routine. Several pages further, just before Caspian begins his journey of escape, Doctor Cornelius instructs Caspian (and us) regarding the reign of terror by which Miraz gained power and currently rules. Between those bookends, the plot reaches a complication in the birth of a son to Miraz, which is the motivation for the king's desire to kill Prince Caspian as his son's rival to the throne.

The last piece of preparation for the journey is a magical Horn that the Doctor places into Caspian's hands. It turns out to be the enchanted Horn that Susan had lost when the Pevensies left Narnia on their previous visit. As an object with magical powers, the Horn belongs to the conventions of the fairy story. But its deeper meaning is a symbolic one, as it represents the presence of divine aid in the world. Further, since it is the means of summoning this supernatural power, it also evidences the qualities of prayer.

Pauline Baynes

When it came time for C. S. Lewis to choose an illustrator for the first of his Narnian books, he turned to a young artist, Pauline Baynes, who had recently illustrated his friend J. R. R. Tolkien's book Farmer Giles of Ham (published in 1949). Ms. Baynes later explained her sense of how the invitation came her way: "C. S. Lewis told me that he had actually gone into a bookshop and asked the assistant there if she could recommend someone who could draw children and animals. I don't know whether he was just being kind to me and making me feel that I was more important than I was or whether he'd simply heard about me from his friend Tolkien." Impressed with the excellent work she did for his first story, Lewis eventually asked that she illustrate all seven of his Narnian chronicles. Though Pauline Baynes consulted with Lewis at various points while she was creating the illustrations, she described him as "the most kindly and tolerant of authors—who seemed happy to leave everything in my completely inexperienced hands! Once or twice I queried the sort of character he had in mind—as with Puddleglum & then he replied, but otherwise he made no remarks or criticisms. . . . I had rather the feeling that, having got the story written down & out of his mind, that the rest was someone else's job, & that he wouldn't interfere."

Pauline Baynes received her art education at both the Farnham School of Art and the Slade School of Fine Art (London). She has had a successful career as an artist, illustrating well over a hundred volumes and winning the Kate Greenaway Award for her illustrations to Grant Uden's Dictionary of Chivalry (1968). Her artistic work is noteworthy for its precision of detail combined with a lyrical sense of color, movement and form. In addition to illustrating the seven Narnian books, she also created a full-color map of Narnia (1971), which now hangs in the Marion E. Wade Center.

All of the foregoing is preparation for the central action of the chapter, the archetypal perilous nighttime *flight of the hero*. It is frivolous to complain that the presence of an archetype robs a given example of its uniqueness. As J. R. R. Tolkien observed on this subject, "Spring is . . . not really less beautiful because we have seen or heard of other like events. . . . Each leaf, of oak and ash and thorn, is a unique embodiment of the pattern. . . . We do not, or need not, despair of painting because all lines must be either straight or curved." In other words, in spite of the commonality shared by archetypal patterns, there is still a magnificence to be found when we are exposed to the distinctive reality of a given instance of an archetype.

Thus, though we have read and viewed many escape stories, the particular details of Caspian's escape are nonetheless unique. A leading task is to assemble the details that comprise this particular escape through the forest. The actual journey receives a mere three paragraphs (though the passage seems much longer than that). To highlight the nightmare quality of the journey, Lewis makes it end with a blow to the head that renders Caspian unconscious.

ᴄ᷉ *For Reflection or Discussion*

The great strength of archetypal criticism is that it allows us to place a given instance of an archetype into the context of literature as a whole. The nuances of Caspian's perilous journey will take on emotional and imaginative resonance if we recall (and perhaps take time to reread) other stories in which an endangered hero flees for his life.

THE RESCUE MOTIF

The second half of the chapter is governed by the conventions of the rescue motif. Caspian's helpless and endangered state is the crisis from which he needs to be rescued. An archetype that lurks in the background is the *mirac-*

ulous protection of the life of the future king.

A rescue story requires a rescuer and a process by which the endangered person is protected and revived from harm. The rescuer in this case is a striking figure of good—the Badger Trufflehunter. As for the means that Trufflehunter produces to revive Prince Caspian, they are enough to make us momentarily forget the danger through which the Prince has just passed—a fire in a fireplace, a cup of something sweet and hot, a bed of heather in a cozy cave. To top it off, the action is dominated by the kindly figures of the Dwarf Trumpkin and the Badger Trufflehunter, loyal adherents to the values and rulers of Old Narnia.

But Lewis springs a surprise on us by including the villainous Dwarf Nikabrik as a member of the rescue party. Whenever Nikabrik says something in his argumentative and contrary way, it unsettles the security and comfort of the rescue motif setting.

⚬ For Reflection or Discussion

The appeal of rescue stories is perennial (and the Bible is an anthology of rescue stories, we might add).

- One way to organize your reading of the second half of this chapter is to analyze the ways in which the events adhere to the pattern of a rescue story. You might wish to recall and reread some favorite rescue stories, such as Moses' rescue from the bulrushes, Daniel from the lions' den, Tom Sawyer and Becky Thatcher from the cave, and Antonio from Shylock's intended murder by Portia's cleverness in the courtroom.

- Whenever the conversation in the cave turns to Old Narnia and present-day Narnia, the effect is that we get more and more clues about a mystery that is gradually being clarified. We can profitably mold those clues into a "progress report" that codifies what we know about the battle between good and evil for control of Narnia.

ℰ 6 ℊ

The People That Lived in Hiding

TRAVELOGUE

The story line of chapter six: The Badger Trufflehunter and the two Dwarfs take Caspian to meet other Old Narnians. It is an idyllic time for the young Prince as he visits many of his new subjects, including the Three Bulgy Bears, Pattertwig the Squirrel, Glenstorm the Centaur and many other Narnians. He is also introduced to the chivalrous and brave Mouse Reepicheep, who proves to be a staunch and significant ally. A decision is made to hold a Council of War at the Dancing Lawn, and on the night before the council Caspian and his companions are happily privileged to become part of the Fauns' moonlight dance.

Every well-told story swings back and forth in a predictable rhythm between tension and its relief—between stress and relaxation. We do not enjoy stories in which the anxiety that is aroused is unrelenting. The title of this chapter might seem to promise still more danger and threat, but instead we get a happy interlude. The opening sentence sets the tone for the entire chapter: "Now began the happiest times that Caspian had ever known."

THE GENRE OF THE TRAVEL STORY

The chapter is organized around the conventions of the travel story. The virtues of that story type are what have made it a favorite with both storytellers and readers from the time of Homer's *Odyssey* and the Bible onward. The conventions of a travel story include the following: a sense of constant movement from one locale to the next; variety of adventure, as something new is almost certain to happen at the next stop on the journey; encounters with a range of interesting characters; the pleasures of descriptive technique, as the storyteller fills us in on the physical settings along the way.

"When Walter Hooper asked where he found the word 'Narnia,' Lewis showed him Murray's Small Classical Atlas, edited G. B. Grundy (1904), which he acquired when he was reading the classics with Mr Kirkpatrick at Great Bookham. On plate 8 of the Atlas is a map of ancient Italy. Lewis had underscored the name of a little town called Narnia, simply because he liked the sound of it. Narnia—or 'Narni' in Italian—is in Umbria, halfway between Rome and Assisi."

ROGER LANCELYN GREEN AND WALTER HOOPER,
C. S. LEWIS: A BIOGRAPHY

After the perilous journey of escape in the preceding chapter, Caspian's journey in this chapter is like a summer holiday trip. Our primary task as we work our way through the chapter is simply to relish the pleasing details that Caspian encounters (and that we encounter with him). The pleasures mainly fall into the following categories: the places themselves; the shifting cast of intriguing characters whom we encounter during the journey; the variety of adventures, climaxing in the dance of the Fauns by moonlight.

Lewis was a master at doling out new things as his stories unfold. What is new in this chapter is the heavy presence of mythical story material. The more heavily marvelous the details become in a fantasy story or fairy tale, the more it moves along a continuum in the direction of myth. Myth is literature at its most profoundly supernatural. Whereas fantasy and fairy stories give us a world that is merely strange, as we move over the continuum toward myth we encounter a transcendent world above the earthly sphere. Myth, moreover, is a meeting ground between religion and literature.

Something like this happens in chapter six. We begin with talking animals such as a friendly Squirrel and the Bulgy Bears, the Seven Brothers of

Shuddering Wood and the five Black Dwarfs. We end with the Centaurs and Fauns. In this progression, fantasy has deepened into myth.

◌ *For Reflection or Discussion*

There are numerous ways to assimilate this chapter, including focusing on the following:

- the conventions of the travel story
- the pleasures of the fairy tale and especially that branch of it that specializes in humanlike animals
- in regard to both of the foregoing, the inventiveness of Lewis's imagination
- evidence for why the critics agree that a leading theme of this book is the elevation of nature
- reflection on why Lewis would have chosen these fantastic and mythical creatures to picture the realm of Aslan and the good

---

℮ 7 ℈

Old Narnia in Danger

PREPARATION FOR BATTLE

The story line of chapter seven: The Council of War on the Dancing Lawn is interrupted by the unexpected arrival of Doctor Cornelius. He has come to warn the Prince that Miraz and his soldiers are hunting for him. Caspian and his forces relocate to Aslan's How, an ancient and sacred site, which is close to the sea and the great woods that the Telmarines so fear. However, Miraz and his men quickly find Caspian's army, and several skirmishes ensue—with increasingly negative results for the

Old Narnians. Things begin to look dire for Caspian's side, and as a result the deci-sion is made to use Susan's enchanted Horn to summon help.

We should note first that this is the fourth and last chapter of the flashback section that began when Trumpkin the Dwarf informed the Pevensie siblings about what was happening in the world to which they had come. Full-fledged battle stories such as *Prince Caspian* unfold according to a predictable pattern: rumors of a coming battle; preparation for battle; a preliminary skirmish; the main battle; outcome in the form of conquest and defeat; aftermath of battle. Chapter seven is devoted to two council scenes, with a brief battle skirmish dividing them.

THE FIRST COUNCIL SCENE

This chapter is dominated by a familiar motif of epic literature known as *the council of war*. The main action at such councils is to consider alternate plans of action for the ensuing battle and then to reach a decision. The deliberation is usually undertaken by the most influential members of the army in-volved, though the rank and file might be present as observers and respon-dents. And of course the meeting must occur in a carefully chosen place with special significance and an imposing aura.

The first council scene takes place on the Dancing Lawn. In a chapter where the action will eventually become dire, the gathering of the creatures for the council is filled with delicious tidbits of humor, such as "sea-sick" Dwarfs who wish they had not agreed to be carried by Wimbleweather the Giant, the preferred courses of action based on the temperamental traits of the creatures who make the respective proposals, and the chattering Squirrel who delays the start of the session by telling everyone to be silent.

The centerpiece of the council is the arrival of Doctor Cornelius with news that the army of Miraz is on the march, having been tipped off to Prince Caspian's escape by the return of his horse. Even here there is room for humor in the brief introduction of Reepicheep, the self-important

Mouse. The Doctor is the authority figure in the deliberations, and his suggestion that the army of Old Narnia move to Aslan's How (or Mound) located on the outskirts of the Great Woods carries the day.

> ### ℃ *For Reflection or Discussion*
> The main things to be explored are the details that contribute to a prevailing tone of optimism and hope, including the humor and the imposing figure of the Doctor. If we were reading the story for the first time, we would not yet know that this optimism is the false dawn before the storm, so we should assimilate it on its own terms.

HOW NOT TO CONDUCT A BATTLE

The action takes an unpleasant turn with the statement that "it was after they had taken up their quarters in and around the How that fortune began to turn against them." The account now turns to the beginning of battle, and we encounter a litany of missteps that characterize the battle action of the good side. In fact, it is a spectacle of ineptitude, which is hardly what we expect or wish. But of course it is a rule of storytelling that things get worse before they get better for the side of the Good. Without that principle being enacted, we would find stories boring.

A particular virtue of Lewis's storytelling is his mastery of the narrative ingredient of surprise. What catches us unaware in the brief story of defeat is that even here we encounter elements of humor, such as the inept and morose Giant Wimbleweather, who splatters others with his tears.

THE SECOND COUNCIL SCENE

A more imposing council scene ends the chapter. It takes place in the secret and magical chamber at the heart of the How, in effect a hideout. The deliberation is conducted by only five leaders—Prince Caspian, Doctor

Illustrations in the Narnian Books

There is no doubt that for many readers of the Narnian books, the illustrations of Pauline Baynes have become inextricably intertwined in their minds with the words of C. S. Lewis. Indeed it is clear that her exquisite drawings have contributed to the success of the series by enhancing the wonder of the stories for countless readers. Because of this, it is important for American readers to realize that many of the original Baynes illustrations that were published in the British editions of the Narnian tales were not included in early U.S. editions. Indeed, in the case of Prince Caspian, there were fifty original drawings, but only thirty of those made it into the American edition. This discrepancy in published illustrations means that those who grew up with the Macmillan hardcover edition were missing out on a significant portion of what young British children were privileged to enjoy.

Fortunately this disparity has been corrected today, as both American and British hardcover editions generally include all the original illustrations. Thus those readers who have copies of Prince Caspian *dating earlier than 1994 may want to take a look at a newer edition and see what they have been missing. But even with the newer volumes, the buyer must still be aware that there is an inconsistent number of illustrations, depending upon the particular edition. For example, those who own paperback copies of* Prince Caspian *will find a range of Baynes drawings included, extending from none to all fifty illustrations. Unfortunately a fairly recent HarperCollins paperback (2005) included no illustrations at all. For the benefit of those who would like to examine their own copy of* Prince Caspian *and determine the extent of the Baynes illustrations, we have included a chart (in Appendix D) that details the original fifty illustrations found in the British first edition, set in comparison to the thirty drawings in the American first edition.*

Even when readers are able to find a newer edition with all fifty drawings, they should be aware that much of the fine detail and liveliness of the Baynes illustrations as printed in the British first edition has been lost. Sadly, subsequent reprintings have been able to reproduce only darker, smudgier and generally smaller drawings.

Cornelius, the Badger Trufflehunter, the Dwarf Trumpkin and the suspect Dwarf Nikabrik. Even more imposing is the fact that the meeting occurs in a room that houses the Stone on which Aslan had been sacrificed.

As is customary in council scenes, the participants initially do not agree among themselves. In fact, council scenes like this are usually debates. In this case the discussion quickly comes to focus on whether or not Caspian should blow the magical Horn that the Doctor gave him when the Prince set out on his perilous journey through the forest. The Horn is the one that Susan inadvertently mislaid when the Pevensie siblings left Narnia on their previous visit.

The Horn obviously carries a significance beyond the literal. When a cleavage develops between those who believe in the Horn's power and those who are scornful that it possesses any supernatural might, we at once come to see the Horn in a religious light. In fact, the Horn is identified with Aslan by both sides in the debate, so that belief and unbelief in the powers of the Horn become indications of religious belief and unbelief in Aslan, who we know from *The Lion, the Witch and the Wardrobe* is metaphoric of Christ.

Once the decision is made to blow the Horn (the motif known as *the magical summons*), further suspense emerges. There is doubt on the part of some as to whether the summons will be effective. And for those who do believe, they still do not know what form of aid will be summoned; they speculate about whether Aslan himself will come or whether instead the four Kings and Queens (Peter, Susan, Edmund and Lucy) from the early days of Narnia will return. And in either case it is unknown *where* Aslan or the Pevensies might arrive, so scouting parties are dispatched to the most likely sites. Trumpkin is sent out in the direction of Cair Paravel, and when he foolishly takes a shortcut, he is captured by the soldiers of Miraz at an outpost. As readers, we already know about that particular circumstance beginning from the point of Trumpkin's landing on the island where the Pevensie siblings are waiting.

ᘓ **For Reflection or Discussion**

Here are good avenues to explore:

- On the plot level, we can first trace the character clashes that occur, including the religious implications of the dispute over whether the Horn has supernatural powers.
- The debate, as well as a small detail such as the Squirrels' eagerness to be off, lends itself to exploring Lewis's skill in characterization. We all are aware that an individual's true self emerges when he or she is under pressure. This chapter is filled with examples of recognizable "human" experience in that regard.
- We can note the elements of suspense and foreshadowing that enter the story at the end of the chapter.

ℰ 8 ℘

How They Left the Island

PREPARATION FOR MISSION

The story line of chapter eight: After Trumpkin finishes telling his tale to the children, they realize that he has little confidence in their ability to aid Caspian. But Peter's plan to prove their battle worthiness to the Dwarf succeeds: Edmund bests Trumpkin in a fencing match, Susan demonstrates that she is the superior archer and Lucy's cordial heals the Dwarf's recent wound. Ashamed of his lack of faith (a skepticism based upon their youthful appearances), Trumpkin gratefully receives the children's help. They set out together by boat for the mainland and their ultimate destination, Aslan's How.

⚜

With this chapter we suddenly leave the flashback scenes and reenter the story of the Pevensies on the island with the Dwarf Trumpkin. The sounding of Susan's Horn is what joins the two plots, since it was the blowing of the Horn that brought the siblings back into Narnia for the purpose of lending aid to Prince Caspian's army. We might seem to be far removed from the battle story that has been brewing as we return to the characters on the island, but if we continue to think in terms of the coming battle as the unifying action of the story, we can see a connection inasmuch as the children will participate in the final battle.

It is a convention of battle stories that warriors need to prove their credentials before entering battle. In the Old Testament, for example, the boy hero David needed to overcome Saul's skepticism about his fighting abilities before Saul allowed him to enter combat against Goliath. So David asserted his credentials (1 Sam 17:31-37).

CHALLENGE AND RESPONSE

The opening two and a half pages of this chapter record the children's astonishment that it was the blowing of Susan's Horn that brought them into Narnia. Once the children have assimilated what happened, Trumpkin unwittingly throws down a gauntlet by assuming that the Horn has failed to bring the hoped-for help because he cannot see that the children represent genuine and significant aid for the coming battle.

The children respond to the challenge with a display of battle prowess. The ensuing scene is a delicious display of superiority by the perceived underdogs over the obtuse and slightly arrogant challenger. Compared to the actual fighting that will follow, this is a mock battle in the comic mode. Its resolution is the good-humored comeuppance of the foolish skeptic, and all that gets wounded is Trumpkin's pride.

JOURNEY TO THE FRONTLINES

With their credentials for warfare established, the children are ready to go off and join the army. Doing so requires a two-day journey, so the travel motif reenters the story. The journey begins in a rowboat, and something deserves to be said at this point about the seriousness with which Lewis regarded the surface details of his stories.

An index to Lewis's attentiveness to the literal details of a story, both as a storyteller and a reader of stories, comes through clearly in a criticism Lewis made of the sixteenth-century humanists. Writes Lewis, "The humanists could not really bring themselves to believe that the poet cared about the shepherds, lovers, warriors, voyages, and battles. They must be only a disguise for something more 'adult.' " In contrast to the humanists, Lewis emphatically *did* care about narrative details.

The story of the journey from the island to the Hill of the Stone Table illustrates this perfectly. The account is filled with details of imagined geography, rowing, eating and sleeping. By offering so many evocative specifics, Lewis carefully shapes and develops his narrative—and thereby aids his reader in seeing, hearing and experiencing the story.

"[In the Narnia stories] we always know what the characters have to eat, whether it is boiled potatoes, marmalade rolls, or the delicate earths favored by the trees; we are told where the children wash . . . , and what kind of bed they have. . . . We know whether the path is slippery shale, soft grass, or steep rocks, so of course we feel that we have walked it. . . . If dropped suddenly into Narnia, careful readers could find the way from Cair Paravel to the Fords of Beruna."

MARGARET PATTERSON HANNAY, *C. S. LEWIS*

For Reflection or Discussion

- It is a time-honored rule of literary criticism that when part of a story seems to be flat and shallow (Lewis's own metaphor for seemingly unpromising story material in an otherwise good story), we need to exercise our ingenuity in demonstrating how effective the passage is after all. (A good example from the history of literary criticism is the way in which Lewis's disparagement of the last two books of Milton's *Paradise Lost* in his book *A Preface to Paradise Lost* produced a flurry of literary commentary that successfully defended that part of Milton's epic.) The foregoing discussion has suggested some ways of seeing the significance of a chapter that seems to be an interlude after the action had been stoking up for a great battle. You might wish to reflect on other avenues to literary appreciation of what Lewis accomplishes in this chapter, such as the humor of the mock battle between the children and Trumpkin, the delicious irony of Trumpkin's not realizing the true nature of the Pevensie children and the descriptive details in the account of the journey.

- It is also helpful to reflect upon the narrative significance of the interlude or pause in the action. How does a stepping back from the action (as we look forward to the coming battle) heighten our anticipation?

- Geography was obviously important to Lewis in this story. It will yield a lot to go through the chapter again, looking at the details of geography and setting.

℮ 9 ℈

What Lucy Saw

ANOTHER PERILOUS JOURNEY

The story line of chapter nine: After a long day of hard rowing under the hot sun, the weary band finally reaches landfall. The next morning they set out through the thick woods but find it difficult to locate a path that will take them in the right direction. Eventually they manage to struggle through to the Rush River, but once there they

find the terrain different from what they remember. Uncertain of which way to pro-
ceed, they have just chosen to go down the gorge when Lucy sees Aslan, who she feels
confident wants them to go up the slope instead. To her distress, the others choose to
disbelieve her, and (with the exception of Edmund) they vote to go down as originally
decided.

We do not need to ask what the Narnia stories would be without the
journey motif: they would be greatly emaciated in contrast to what they
are *with* the journeys included. But Lewis's reliance on the journey motif is
no more pronounced than the element of journeying is with all the master
storytellers. Journeys allow for testing of character, for variety of adventure, for conflict and the mastery of it, for progress toward a goal, for descriptive excellence, for such narrative staples as suspense and danger.
Specifically, in this chapter, the goal of the journey is to find the Great
River, which in turn will lead to Aslan's How, where Caspian's army is waiting for help.

THE JOURNEY AS PHYSICAL REALITY

The journey on which we accompany Trumpkin and the four Pevensies in
this chapter exists on two levels—the physical and the spiritual. On the literal level, the characters pursue a physical journey toward the meeting point
with Prince Caspian and his army. Two chief ingredients constitute the heart
of this particular journey. One is the physical hardships of the journey on
foot. Because (as previously noted) Lewis took the surface details of literature seriously, he was a master at creating journeys that fully engage our
imagination and emotions.

The second ingredient that makes this journey come alive on its literal
level is the uncertainty of the characters on the journey regarding how to
reach their destination. As a result, the story becomes a suspense story. In
fact, Peter announces at one point, "We're lost." To make matters worse, the

majority of the party decides to go down the gorge, which is the wrong direction for them to take. The chapter ends on a heart-rending note: "Lucy came last of the party, crying bitterly."

"[Lewis] was a superb stylist, one of the most articulate of twentieth-century writers, excelling in both logical, analytical adeptness and creative, imaginative expression."

ROLLAND HEIN, *CHRISTIAN MYTHMAKERS*

THE JOURNEY AS SPIRITUAL INDEX

As the title of the chapter hints, there is also a spiritual level of significance to the journey. This is true because Aslan enters the action, and a cleavage develops between those who see Aslan and those who do not.

Because Aslan is a Lion who represents the Narnian incarnation of Christ (based upon what we know from *The Lion, the Witch and the Wardrobe*), to see Aslan means to be in touch with God. And not to see him is to be out of touch with God. This is the religious level of meaning, which Peter Schakel interprets as follows: "What a person sees depends on who he or she is and what he or she is looking for. . . . Because Lucy's companions do not believe Aslan is present, they do not see him." At a literary level, Lucy's position is an adolescent version of a venerable archetype known as *the spurned woman*. In that motif our sympathy is evoked for a female character who is unfairly rejected and scorned by one or more other characters. Storytellers love the motif because of its predictable emotional impact.

ℭℯ *For Reflection or Discussion*

The foregoing commentary has suggested the two primary ways to assimilate this chapter:

- One is to relive and relish the imagined details of the journey, including its growing dangers. It is a perilous journey par excellence, replete with not only conflict with external surroundings but also character clashes within the traveling community.

- The second line of inquiry is to explore the religious meaning of faith and doubt regarding Aslan and his will. Lucy sees Aslan and knows that the right path is up the gorge; the characters who do not see Aslan take the wrong direction, down the gorge. It is part of the mystique of this story that such a simple narrative detail as this can embody so much religious meaning.
- Peter Schakel offers an original slant on the motif of seeing Aslan (which will occur in subsequent chapters as well as this one) by suggesting that characters in the story see Aslan only after they believe in him. This remains a provocative possibility, but the text does not actually tip its hand in that direction. It is also possible that characters in the story believe in Aslan only after seeing him. You might wish to examine closely the scenes in which characters come to see Aslan and reach your own conclusion on this point.

℃ 10 ℈

The Return of the Lion

A FAIRY STORY AND MORE

The story line of chapter ten: Going down the gorge proves to be even more difficult than the travelers' earlier trek through the woods. When they eventually make it out and are almost to the Fords of Beruna, they unexpectedly encounter Miraz's sentries and are forced to make a speedy retreat all the way back uphill to where they began. That evening, Lucy awakens from a deep sleep and hears Aslan calling her name. Walking into the moonlit woods, she makes her way through the awak-

ening Trees until she finds the Great Lion. Lucy's joy at being reunited with Aslan
is dimmed, however, when he instructs her to awaken the others and tell them that
they must leave at once.

As the journey to find the Great River unfolds for yet another chapter, it takes on the magnitude of an epic journey. The grand nature of the action is reinforced by the presence of the standard epic motif of a human-divine encounter. Because of the past history of Lucy and Aslan in *The Lion, the Witch and the Wardrobe,* the account of their memorable nighttime encounter makes the story above all a reunion story.

REVERSING COURSE

Chapter ten falls into two distinct halves. The first half continues the journey of the five unfortunates in their quest to find Prince Caspian at Aslan's How. Lewis obviously had his imagined geography clear in his mind. Even if we struggle to picture the details of the journey, the account wins us with its portrayal of physical hardships. J. R. R. Tolkien praised fairy stories for their ability to put us in touch with elemental physical reality: "It was in fairy-stories that I first divined the potency . . . and wonder of things, such as stone, and wood, and iron; tree and grass; house and fire; bread and wine." The journeying in *Prince Caspian* illustrates Tolkien's point perfectly.

The journeying half of chapter ten ends with an unexpected intrusion of the battle motif, as the group is attacked by soldiers of Miraz stationed at an outpost. The effect is not only to infuse added voltage into the account of hardships but also to remind us of the overall story that unifies the book—the eventual showdown between the forces of evil in the world and the spiritual kingdom of Aslan and his followers. Furthermore, the attack is actually a providential intervention from Aslan: it is the event that forces the group to reverse direction and go up the gorge instead of down it, as Aslan and his representative Lucy had earlier insisted.

> ## ℭℯ *For Reflection or Discussion*
> Since the second half of the chapter will shift gears so drastically, we can profitably take stock of the first half before moving on. A good avenue to organizing our experience of the journey down the gorge and then up it is simply to ponder the qualities that make this particular journey a literary success. What are the details that make this journey come to life for you?

THE UPRIGHT SHALL BEHOLD HIS FACE (PSALM 11:7)

The rest of the chapter is devoted to Lucy's solitary nighttime trip into the woods to encounter the Lion Aslan. Aslan is the representative of Christ in the Narnia stories. Therefore to encounter and embrace the Lion is to encounter and embrace Christ. These are the assumptions with which we must read the story of Lucy's journey into the woods.

It becomes clear at once that this is one of Lewis's inspired passages. It is suffused with a sense of the numinous or holy. We must begin by being alive to the captivating nature of the literal narrative details—to the moon, the starry sky, the forest landscape with its moving trees, the circle of grass with a welcoming Lion in the middle of it.

At such a point we need to heed Lewis's own advice that a fairy tale such as this requires a double response—a childlike response and (for adult readers) an adult response. Lewis said this in connection with Edmund Spenser's long poem *The Faerie Queene:* "It demands of us a child's love of marvels. . . . It is of course much more than a fairy-tale, but unless we can enjoy it as a fairy-tale first of all, we shall not really care for it."

But once we have relished the magical fairy-tale qualities of the scene, we need to ponder its spiritual meaning as well. Even more than in *The Lion, the Witch and the Wardrobe,* Lucy is the spiritual hero of the story, though the space allotted to her is modest. Peter Schakel suggests that in *Prince Caspian* the adage that "seeing is believing" is reversed, so that to believe is to see. So Lucy's excursion is an exercise of spiritual faith.

Much of the religious meaning of *Prince Caspian* is embodied in the relationship between Lucy and Aslan. And an important part of that, in turn, is the motif of Aslan's insistence that Lucy follow him, if necessary by herself. This theme of Aslan's (Christ's) individual call takes two forms in the encounter between the Great Lion and Lucy in this chapter—first, a rebuke that Lucy did not part company with her fellow travelers, and second, Aslan's immediate command to Lucy to follow him even if the others refuse to do so.

In a letter to a young reader Lewis explained the source for the name of Aslan: "I found the name in the notes to Lane's Arabian Nights: it is the Turkish for Lion. I pronounce it Ass-lan myself. And of course I meant the Lion of Judah."

C. S. LEWIS, *LETTERS TO CHILDREN*

Lucy's reunion with Aslan telescopes outward into her having to awaken her traveling companions and to get them to see Aslan or, failing that, to follow Aslan's instructions nonetheless. This scene is still part of the encounter with Aslan, and its function is to show Lucy in the role of witness to unbelieving companions. At the plot level, it is a conflict of high intensity. At the religious level, the issue is the ultimate one—belief in God and the supernatural versus unbelief.

For Reflection or Discussion

This episode will yield a wealth of spiritual meanings if pondered from the following vantage points:

- the character of Aslan (representing Christ) as seen in his interactions with Lucy

- what Lucy learns about the life of faith as gleaned from the Lion's instructions to her and her interactions with Aslan
- the theme of the two worlds—how people in this world can relate to God and the unseen spiritual world
- the experience of witnessing to a skeptical society
- the sharp contrast between people who live by their encounter with God and those who have not seen or do not believe in God
- the outworking of the theme of Aslan's (Christ's) call to individuals to follow him

ℰ 11 ℐ

The Lion Roars

EPIPHANY

The story line of chapter eleven: With great reluctance Peter, Susan, Edmund and the Dwarf Trumpkin agree to accompany Lucy as she follows Aslan. The nighttime walk is far from pleasant, as all are weary and irritable, and there is genuine nervousness as they walk along the edge of the gorge with only the moonlight to show them their footing. At first none of the others can see Aslan—only Lucy can do so. But she perseveres in following Aslan nonetheless, and after a time Edmund glimpses him as well. Peter is the next one to see the Great Lion. Eventually even the Dwarf and Susan are able to see Aslan. With Aslan's assistance, they arrive at the Great Mound, where Caspian's forces are camped. The boys and Trumpkin are sent inside the Mound, while the girls remain with Aslan and become part of a boisterous celebration with Bacchus and other mythic creatures.

Storytellers have used the narrative device of epiphany from time im-memorial, but it was twentieth-century fiction writer James Joyce who popularized the term as used in a literary context. The word *epiphany* means revelation or manifestation. The original usage was religious and referred to an appearance and recognition of deity. Drawing upon his own Catholic background, James Joyce used the word to refer to that moment late in a short story where the main insight of the story is rec-ognized by one or more characters in the story and by the reader as well. Book-length stories might have multiple moments of epiphany. Both the religious and literary meanings of epiphany dominate chapter eleven of *Prince Caspian*.

SEEING ASLAN ONE BY ONE

Chapter ten ended with a brief scene in which Lucy's siblings refused to be-lieve her account of having seen Aslan, since none of *them* could see him. Storytelling conventions being what they are, we could predict that this con-flict would be the main narrative motif for at least the first half of the next chapter, and that is exactly what we find.

For two and a half pages we relive Lucy's misery in not being believed in her claim about seeing Aslan. The backdrop for this action is Aslan's state-ment near the end of the preceding chapter that the others might not believe Lucy, "certainly not at first." In that same earlier scene, Aslan had told Lucy to follow him, if necessary alone. That is what happens in the present scene: Aslan walks at a slow pace, and Lucy keeps her eyes on him as the others follow, even though initially they do not see him. Storytellers love to give us variations on a theme, with changes introduced into a basic pattern. In this scene the motif of the perilous nighttime journey is transformed by the pres-ence of Aslan as a guide.

Once the journey is well under way, Lewis introduces the technique of epiphany. One by one, Edmund, Peter and Susan come to see Aslan, with varying degrees of remorse for having doubted Lucy's word. Lucy's extended reunion with Aslan having been narrated in the previous chapter, the others are now reunited with Aslan with appropriate individual touches. That leaves the Dwarf Trumpkin to be resolved of his unbelief, and it is a memorable scene, with the Lion tossing the Dwarf into the air at a climactic point.

Mythological Characters in Prince Caspian

The chapter numbers indicate the chapters in which the characters first appear in the story.

- Bacchus: Roman god of nature, wine and revelry (chapter 11)
- Dryads: Female tree spirits of Greek mythology, protectors of forests (chapter 4)
- Hamadryads: Similar to Dryads but unable to move about as freely since their life is connected to an individual tree (chapter 9)
- Jinn: In Islamic mythology, a supernatural evil spirit that—usually in response to a summons—appears to people in human, animal or hybrid form (chapter 8)
- Maenads: Frolicsome women who accompany Bacchus (chapter 14)
- Naiads: Female water spirits of Greek mythology (chapter 4)
- Pomona: Roman goddess of gardens and orchards (chapter 2)
- Silenus: The elderly but boisterous foster father and tutor of Bacchus, learned in the secrets of nature and compared to Socrates by the ancients (chapter 11)

A PARTY IN THE MYTHICAL MODE

The second half of the chapter is an extended epiphany. When Aslan roars, a crowd of mythical creatures comes running. The chaotic celebration scene is identified as "a Romp." Eventually refreshments in the form of luscious grapes overtake the festivities.

For readers whose ideas of narrative are those of realistic fiction, it may be hard to enter into the spirit of what is happening in this scene. However, those acquainted with contemporary fantasy literature will find this scene tame by modern standards. For still other readers familiar with the old mythical stories such as Edmund Spenser's *Faerie Queene,* what happens in this chapter is par for the course. The weird creatures are the stock-in-trade of mythical stories. Our forebears of long ago loved them and regarded the classical myths as "old memories, old dreams, old shapes of loveliness." The old mythical creatures were often wild creatures, as much animal as human. In chapter eleven of *Prince Caspian* they are an extension of the pastoral (rural) identity of the celebration scene. Given the mythical tradition that underlies the scene, *of course* the party will occur on a grassy plain and *of course* the refreshments will be grapes.

"Lewis believed fairy tales and religion were naturally connected. He saw myths and legends as a step in humankind's development of belief. To him, they were part of a logical path to Christianity. When lecturing [to] his university students about the . . . epic poem The Faerie Queene *(1590) by Edmund Spenser, [Lewis] said: 'Anywhere in this wood . . . you may hear angels singing—or come upon satyrs romping. What is more, the satyrs may lead you to the angels.' (Spenser's* Images of Life, *96) . . . Lewis didn't mind that the path through paganism was muddy."*

DAVID COLBERT, *THE MAGICAL WORLDS OF NARNIA*

℺ *For Reflection or Discussion*

It is always a profitable exercise to ask what function a given scene or chapter plays in an ongoing story. Ostensibly this chapter is an interlude between the ordeal of the journey to find Aslan's How and the impending battle. But such an interlude needs to fit into the narrative motifs and religious themes that dominate the story as a whole. What are those motifs and themes?

ℰ 12 ℮

Sorcery and Sudden Vengeance

EVIL COUNCIL CONVENED

The story line of chapter twelve: After Trumpkin and the two boys have made their way through the corridors of the Mound, they pause to listen outside the Central Chamber, where an angry conversation is taking place between, on the one hand, Caspian and his loyal advisers and, on the other hand, Nikabrik and his shadowy friends. The argument eventually escalates into a deadly struggle, and Peter, Edmund and Trumpkin rush in to aid the Old Narnians. Together they overcome their evil adversaries, who turn out to be a Hag and a Wer-Wolf—in addition to the traitorous Dwarf Nikabrik.

The main story pattern in this chapter is the council scene, and within that genre it is an example of attempted fraudulent or evil counsel. It is a familiar story type from the ancient past and from genres like epic and fairy story that perpetuate the patterns of what earlier eras quaintly called "the antique world."

In Dante's *Inferno,* sinners who receive the worst punishment in hell include those who offered fraudulent counsel and those who were traitors to their party and leaders. Chapter twelve enacts a Dantesque scenario in which bad counsel is narrowly defeated by forces of good.

BAD COUNSEL PROPOSED

The chapter opens with Trumpkin, Peter and Edmund entering the passageway of Aslan's How. We suddenly remember that the four chapters dealing with the children's journey from Cair Paravel to Aslan's How have diverted us from the main plot—the story of Caspian's conflict against the forces of

Miraz. Chapter seven (just before the interjected story of the journey from Cair Paravel to Aslan's How) had ended with a council scene set inside Aslan's Mound, and we now return to a follow-up council scene in the same location. We arrive in the midst of the meeting along with Trumpkin, Peter and Edmund, with whom we overhear the proceedings.

This council has been occasioned by the opening defeat of the army of Prince Caspian by the forces of Miraz. The Old Narnians need help, and at this point we remember that it has taken the Pevensies two days to make their journey. The initial topic of discussion at the council is therefore the problem posed by the failure of help to arrive even though the magical Horn has been blown.

Faced with the problem, Nikabrik is ready to propose a radical alternative to waiting for help to arrive. He has brought two cohorts to the meeting—a Hag and a Wer-Wolf, conventional mythical creatures and figures of repulsive evil. As the conversation unfolds, Nikabrik emerges as the archetypal traitor. He is not just a common traitor either. He expresses scorn for the very things that are the foundation of Old Narnia, including loyalty to Aslan and the king. Additionally he proposes summoning the ghost of the White Witch from the dead. What Nikabrik attempts is a coup.

BAD COUNSEL DEFEATED

Just as the rituals of sorcery and necromancy are beginning to unfold, a makeshift fight occurs in which Nikabrik, the Hag and the Wer-Wolf are defeated by Caspian, Trumpkin, Peter and Edmund. The skirmish is narrated briefly but vividly and with an evocation of the grotesque with such details as a dead Hag from which Peter quickly turns his eyes and the command to fling "the vermin" (the Hag and Wer-Wolf) into a pit. But there are images of courage and honor as well, and some of the battle motifs embedded in the story draw upon very old motifs. For example, when we read regarding Caspian's wound that "cleaning and bandaging the wound took a long time," this hints at an ancient conviction that wounds suffered in battle were a badge of great honor.

Some of the characters who joined the fray had not even been introduced to each other yet, so introductions ensue as Peter and Edmund are brought into the circle of Old Narnians for the first time. We round out the tumultuous event by reenacting an action that is dear to children's literature—eating breakfast. Looking back over the action, it is obvious that the chapter has been built around the archetypal narrow escape and rescue.

ℭ *For Reflection or Discussion*

Several good approaches to this chapter exist:

- Evocation of fear and terror is a standard ingredient of fairy stories. A literary critic speaks of "design for terror" as a common strategy. One way to organize this chapter is to tabulate the specific ingredients of Lewis's design for terror.
- Second, for all the far-flung fantasy of the action, it embodies a wealth of recognizable human experiences. This is seen especially at the level of characterization, and it is always important to keep looking at the characters in a story as embodying much of what the storyteller wants to say about life.
- Lewis shows great skill in delineating how the forces of evil can infiltrate a situation and turn the tide of affairs to their own evil ends.

ℭ 13 ℈

The High King in Command

CHALLENGE TO SINGLE COMBAT

The story line of chapter thirteen: Having quelled an internal revolt, High King Peter now turns his attention to Miraz and his army. Since the Old Narnians have little hope of winning a battle against Miraz's army, Peter decides to challenge the usurper king to single combat. He sends Edmund, the Giant Wimbleweather and Glenstorm

the Centaur to carry the challenge to Miraz. Though it is not to his advantage to accept the challenge (since his army clearly outnumbers Caspian's forces), Miraz is
tricked into accepting Peter's challenge through the treacherous scheming of his own
disloyal counselors.

There have been plenty of reminders throughout the story that the overall
point of unity in the story is the struggle for control of Narnia. We have been
given hints all along that the story will eventually become a battle story. There
have been skirmishes along the way, but the climactic battle keeps being de-
layed. With chapter thirteen we are finally moving toward the great battle.

PLAYING BY THE RULES

In older literature such as epic and romance (including the Arthurian stories),
battles are carried out by an elaborate set of rules and conventions. Features
of battle protocol run away with Lewis's story in this chapter and the next.

The rules of ancient warfare allowed for the outcome of the struggle to be
determined by single combat between representatives from each side,
thereby eliminating mass slaughter in battle. This rule is the frame of reference for what happens in this chapter. The sequence of action unfolds as follows: Peter composes a formal challenge; the challenge is delivered to Miraz
in his camp; Miraz's counselors trick him into accepting the challenge by
urging him to decline it; when news of the acceptance arrives at Aslan's How,
Caspian's advisers start planning for the implementation of the duel.

> ### For Reflection or Discussion
> A good way to assimilate a chapter like this is to relish the "otherness"
> of the world that we enter as we read. Part of this can consist of tabu-
> lating the specific elements of martial protocol that are foreign to our
> own experience. Surprisingly, the chapter is one of Lewis's comic mas-
> terpieces; noting the instances of humor is a fruitful exercise.

The Map for Prince Caspian

Unfortunately, not only did the first American edition of Prince Caspian *reduce the number of illustrations included, but also it omitted the endpaper map that Pauline Baynes had prepared at C. S. Lewis's request. So intentional was Lewis about this that he explained in a letter of January 8, 1951, exactly what he had in mind: "My idea was that the map should be more like a medieval map than an Ordnance Survey—mountains and castles drawn—perhaps winds blowing at the corners—and a few heraldic-looking ships, whales and dolphins in the sea. Aslan gazing at the moon would make an excellent cover design (to be repeated somewhere in the book; but do as you please about that.)" Fortunately this map has been restored to current hardcover editions of* Prince Caspian, *and it is now easier to read since it has been relocated from the endpapers to inside pages.*

℮ 14 ℈

How All Were Very Busy

CONQUEST STORY

The story line of chapter fourteen: The High King Peter engages Miraz in single combat. As first Peter and then Miraz gets the upper hand, the two combatants are surrounded on all sides by alternately cheering and anxious spectators: Caspian's Old Narnians and the opposing Telmarine army. The fight is finally decided by the continuing treachery of Miraz's men, who stab their fallen leader and attempt to blame Peter. Battle between the armies ensues, but when the Awakened Trees rush forward in their full fury and strength, the Telmarines flee in terror. Meanwhile Aslan and the girls are liberating others who have been living in various sorts of bondage.

I is a rule of storytelling that a reader's expectations are partly fulfilled (since without the familiar narrative conventions storytelling would not be possible) and partly denied (since total compliance with expectations would bore a good reader). In this chapter devoted to the climax of the battle we get a combination of the expected and the surprising.

SINGLE COMBAT

A single combat having been agreed to, we now observe it. The combatants are Peter and Miraz, and the exchange between Edmund and Peter at the end of the preceding chapter highlights the thing that makes the combat interesting to us, namely, its uncertainty of outcome. Peter is indeed fighting to find out if he can win.

With this as the premise, the duel emerges as a good one—a self-respecting single combat. Lewis's premise in constructing the event was the usual one of fluctuation in battle. At one moment the initiative lies with Peter; at the next moment, with Miraz. This back-and-forth rhythm, with a rest between the first two rounds (British *bouts*), makes the account a textbook case of how to write a single combat story. At some point the villainous combatant is supposed to wrestle the hero down and sit on top of him, as Grendel's monstrous mother does to Beowulf. Miraz does it to Peter, and Peter barely escapes decapitation. The combat meets all the right criteria, being "most horrible and most magnificent" at the same time.

ATTACK OF THE TREES

Just as the single combat is proceeding according to form, Lewis springs some major surprises on us. When Miraz slips, three treacherous Telmarines enter the ring to attack Peter on the false pretense that Peter had stabbed Miraz in the back. One of the three, moreover, stabs Miraz to death. General battle between the two sides is joined, but before the fighting can assume full magnitude, the Telmarines are routed and begin to retreat. They surren-

---

The *derivation of the name of the ruling Telmarines (who include King Miraz and his nephew Prince Caspian) is explained well by Walter Hooper as follows:* "The word Tellus comes from the Latin and in Roman mythology means the goddess of the Earth. It is also a name for the Earth and its inhabitants. Mare in Latin means sea, and it is from this word that we get marine. 'Telmar,' thus, means earth-sea, and 'Telmarines' are 'Sailors from the Earth' or 'Earthly sailors,' as explained by Aslan at the end of the book."

WALTER HOOPER, *COMPANION AND GUIDE*

---

der when they discover that the bridge over the Great River has disappeared.

It is a commonplace that in *Prince Caspian* Lewis raises numerous narrative expectations and then denies those expectations rather than fulfilling them. Obviously, for this story, Lewis elevated surprise as a principle of plot over the principle of anticipation and fulfillment. The account of the defeat of the Telmarines in chapter fourteen contains multiple examples. For one thing, a single combat is not supposed to end in general warfare, nor is one of the duelists supposed to be killed by his own soldiers.

Furthermore, the narrative premise throughout the story has been that we are moving toward a climactic battle scene in the epic and romance modes. Lewis *does* give us a climactic encounter on the battlefield, but not in the form of a full-scale military encounter. The battle is over almost as soon as it begins, and it is not won through superior military prowess. Instead Lewis composed a kind of spoof. Part of the Telmarines' degeneracy is their isolation from nature, as seen (for example) in their fear of trees and water. As a result, when the Trees start to move in the battle scene of chapter fourteen, the Telmarines panic and conclude that the end of the world has come. They are thus victims of their own folly and phobia, not of military defeat.

ℭₑ *For Reflection or Discussion*

The impressionistic question is always appropriate for a battle scene: for you, personally, what makes this a good or bad battle scene? In a letter Lewis once wrote, "Spenser, like all the Elizabethan poets, is bad at fights." How does Lewis himself escape that stricture in this scene?

ASLAN'S VICTORY ROMP

The disappearance of the bridge requires an explanation, so Lewis gives it to us in the second half of the chapter, answering his own question, "But what had happened to the bridge?" We get a flashback that narrates what Aslan had accomplished since daybreak on the day of the battle. The account is a tour de force of mythological invention.

The main motif is announced by Aslan at the start. "We will make holiday," he says to Lucy and Susan. But it is not an ordinary holiday. With the girls riding on Aslan's back, a procession of mythological creatures sets off for the river to deliver the river god of his chains, that is, the bridge. After the bridge has crashed down, the revelers wade through the river and enter the town on the other side.

Satire enters the story of Aslan's trip through the town and countryside on the other side of the river. The key to interpreting what is happening is to be aware that the territory has been in long bondage to "new" Narnia, a state where oppression of individuals (especially children) is the chief reality. In the mode of other satirists, Lewis uses the technique of caricature in portraying the citizens of that world, and Aslan plays practical jokes on them. But then the tone shifts as Aslan heals a child's ill aunt and Bacchus turns water into wine. Suddenly we have entered the world of the New Testament Gospels and their accounts of Jesus' miracles. In addition Lewis uses this sequence to tie up a loose thread from previously in the story line when the

Bacchus in Narnia

One of the most baffling aspects of Prince Caspian for modern readers (and perhaps especially for Christian readers) is the prominence that Lewis gives to the classical god Bacchus. We can say right off that Lewis was a specialist in Renaissance literature, and for Renaissance authors and readers the mythological characters and stories of the past were old forms of loveliness that appealed to their imaginations.

Bacchus was the god of wine and fertility. In his grossest form he was a drunkard who led frenzied women known as Maenads on wild nighttime processions known as bacchanals. But Bacchus did not always appear in his grossest form in literary handlings of the myth. The fact that Lewis puts Bacchus into Aslan's celebratory march shows that Lewis intended to Christianize this pagan god, making him respectable rather than debauched. We get a hint of this at the conclusion of chapter eleven, at the end of Aslan's Romp, when Susan says, "I wouldn't have felt safe with Bacchus and all his wild girls if we'd met them without Aslan," to which Lucy replies, "I should think not."

At his most respectable, Bacchus came to represent liberation, nature, enthusiasm and celebration. A close reading of his actions in the victory procession of chapter fourteen will reveal that these are the values Lewis wished to embody in him. It is also possible that Lewis intended to assert by narrative means that Aslan can redeem even the wildest impulses.

healed woman turns out to be Caspian's earlier-banished Nurse, now deposited before him on the battlefield.

If we stop to recall that this chapter began with Peter entering the arena to engage in single combat with Miraz, the amount of action has been breathtaking. Everything has been connected, though, by the genre at work in the chapter, that of the conquest story. The Telmarines have been conquered in two complementary ways—by the army on the battlefield and by the victory march of Aslan and his mythological entourage.

℃ **For Reflection or Discussion**

The episode of Aslan's Romp is governed by a mood of high-spiritedness. Identifying the details that you liked best is an avenue toward literary analysis of the episode.

℃ 15 ℃

Aslan Makes a Door in the Air

DENOUEMENT

The story line of chapter fifteen: The defeated Telmarine army surrenders to Aslan at the Fords of Beruna. Caspian meets the Great Lion for the first time and is proclaimed King of Narnia. The victory of the Old Narnians is celebrated with a great and glorious feast provided by Aslan through the magic of Bacchus and his friends. Following the celebration, all the Telmarine people (including the imprisoned army) are offered the choice of remaining in Narnia and accepting the rule of Caspian and the Talking Beasts, Dwarfs and other mythic creatures—or being sent to another home provided by Aslan. Many of the older Telmarines choose to leave (rather than submit to the rule of others), and following the lead of Peter, Susan, Edmund and Lucy (who are returning to England), they all go through the magical temporary doorway that Aslan has created.

All well-made plots end with *denouement,* a French word that means "tying up of loose ends." Lewis crams his last chapter with an abundance of action, but the one thing that all the events have in common is that they are the aftermath to the conquest that occupied the previous chapter. To elevate just one of the events to the status of title is a solemn joke that Lewis plays on his readers, as though the chapter has just one main event.

A BUSY DAY FOR ASLAN

The chapter is structured as a pageant of separate scenes in which an individual or group appears before Aslan. The first of these is the presentation of Prince Caspian before Aslan to be declared King of Narnia. This brings the story of the titular character of the book to its conclusion.

Lewis was so captivated by his invention of Reepicheep that he devoted a whopping four pages to the mouse, chiefly focusing on his quest to have his tail restored. Then various heroes of the war are elevated to high-sounding positions,

A Fascination with Mice

C. S. Lewis had a great love for animals of all sorts throughout his life, but he had a particular fascination with mice that began in childhood and extended into his adult years. As a young child, he had a much-loved black and white pet mouse named Tommy. In August 1907, after a visit to the London zoo with her two sons, Lewis's mother, Flora, wrote home that the boys "were both delighted with the animals, and we actually saw some mice that were almost the same as common ones. I think Jack [Lewis's family nickname] was as much pleased with them as with anything we saw." Many of his own childhood writings, which were called the Boxen stories, including his History of Mouse-land, were filled with characters that were mice. Even as an adult, Lewis's affection for the small creatures endured. Writing to a young child about his Narnian character, the heroic mouse Reepicheep, Lewis declared: "I love real mice. There are lots in my rooms in College but I have never set a trap. When I sit up late working they poke their heads out from behind the curtains just as if they were saying, 'Hi! Time for you to go to bed. We want to come out and play.' " Mice also appear in the final volume of Lewis's space trilogy, That Hideous Strength, when they are fed bread crumbs by the Director (Ransom) in his room—something Lewis acknowledged doing in his own Oxford rooms.

and the rebellious Telmarine soldiers are imprisoned. Poetic justice is the governing narrative principle, as the good are rewarded and the evil punished.

The mythological impulse is never far from the surface in *Prince Caspian,* and Lewis turns to it for a final fling in the next sequence. With a gigantic campfire roaring, mythological beings create a sumptuous feast whose ingredients are named in evocative catalogs of foods. Lewis apparently liked

Departures Home

Here is how C. S. Lewis chose to describe the moment of transition—the moment when his characters must leave Narnia and return to their own fictional "real world"—in each of his seven children's stories.

- The Lion, the Witch and the Wardrobe *(1950). After spending some years in Narnia, during which time the children grow up into young adults, the four Kings and Queens are riding through the woods in pursuit of a wild white stag when they stumble upon the lamp-post and find their way back through the wardrobe into the spare room in the Professor's house, where they are once again young children (and no longer kings and queens).*

- Prince Caspian *(1951). The four children (Peter, Susan, Edmund and Lucy) return to their own world through a doorway made out of three stakes of wood that Aslan orders constructed in a forest glade. Before walking through this doorway, Peter and Susan are alerted that they are now too old to remain in Narnia and will not be able to return in the future. Lucy and Edmund are not so warned. Once having walked through the doorway, the children find themselves back on the same country railway station where this particular journey to Narnia began.*

- The Voyage of the "Dawn Treader" *(1952). Lucy and Edmund are told that this will be their last time in Narnia (although Eustace will return). Their return to the normal world is by way of a door that Aslan creates for them far up above in the blue sky. Upon returning, Lucy and Edmund find themselves back once more in the guest bedroom in Eustace's Cambridge* how things were unfolding, for he devoted a whole paragraph to describing the soils that the Trees received to eat. Comic U-shaped plots (stories that descend into potential tragedy and then rise to a happy ending) typically end with either a feast or a wedding, and Lewis gives us the first. There is a picturesque paragraph describing how the partiers gradually fall off to sleep instead of getting up and going away.

- **The Silver Chair (1953).** *Aslan blows Eustace and Jill away from Narnia and back to the Mountain of Aslan (where their adventure first began). Here they watch Aslan bring King Caspian back to life. Caspian is then given permission to return with Eustace and Jill to their own world for a brief time to help them teach the bullies of their boarding school, Experiment House, a lesson. They return to their world through a gap in the school wall, which was knocked down by Aslan's tremendous roar.*

- **The Horse and His Boy (1954).** *Because all the action within this story takes place during the time period when the four children (Peter, Susan, Edmund and Lucy) reigned as Kings and Queens over the inhabitants of Narnia during the final pages of* The Lion, the Witch and the Wardrobe, *there is no transition into or out of Narnia.*

- **The Magician's Nephew (1955).** *Though the children used magic rings to enter Narnia, they need no magic to return home because Aslan is with them. Aslan first accompanies the children to the "Wood between the Worlds." And then, after simply looking into his face, the children find themselves transported home as a result of Aslan's mighty power.*

- **The Last Battle (1956).** *In this final story in the Narnian chronicles, the seven friends of Narnia, children from the earlier stories, find themselves unexpectedly inside a stable in Narnia. Once there, they discover to their amazed delight that the stable's inside is much bigger than its outside, for they are no longer in Narnia. At long last they have entered Aslan's own country ("further up and further in"), a great land that contains all they have ever loved—a land where the real Narnia and the real England exist side by side forever. There will be no more transitions. They are home at last.*

Something remains to be done with the rebellious Telmarines. Aslan delivers them an ultimatum: they either have to agree to live under King Caspian and the rules of Old Narnia (an option most of the young accept) or be transported to their native land far from Narnia, which turns out to be earth (an offer that many of the older men choose).

> ### ℂℯ *For Reflection or Discussion*
> A story as told is always the product of conscious choices on the part of the storyteller. Lewis consciously put the diverse material noted above into this concluding chapter. We can theorize and speculate about what these particular details are doing here.

GOING HOME

The story of the Telmarines who walked through a door from Narnia to their original homeland is now followed by the moment that we knew from the outset would need to come—the return of the Pevensie siblings from Narnia to the railway station. Surely, whenever this thought has crossed our mind, we have been dismayed to consider that the children would eventually have to leave Narnia once again.

The narrative motifs at work at the end of *Prince Caspian* are leave-taking and farewell, with the accompanying emotions of resignation and sadness. All the details can be related to those motifs and feelings. In the niceties of farewell we catch echoes of what has happened earlier in the story (for example, the references to the Bulgy Bears and Trumpkin and Trufflehunter). More than that, though, we relive the universal human experience of hurriedly leaving behind a place and a set of experiences that have occurred in that place. The thought of Peter and Susan never returning to Narnia makes the emotions all the more piercing.

ℭ *For Reflection or Discussion*

Late in the book Edmund and Lucy are dismayed at the thought that Peter and Susan will never return to Narnia. They are our representatives at that moment, expressing the longing we feel toward Narnia and the story that Lewis has just told us about it. Taking our cue from this longing we feel toward Narnia, we can consider the conclusion of the story a good time to take a look back at the story and our experience of it. Here are some avenues toward reflection or discussion:

- What are the ways in which the imagined world of Narnia has a hold on us? Why do we value the world Lewis has created?

- What are the story qualities of *Prince Caspian* that you would rate as being important parts of the book's greatness? More generally, what is Lewis best at as a storyteller?

- What commonalities can be observed between the imagined world of Narnia and our own world? As part of that, what universal human experiences have been memorably embodied in *Prince Caspian*?

- The Christian orientation of the book is seen primarily in the Christ figure of Aslan and in the moral models that the story offers for approval and disapproval. What religious and moral meanings are most important in this story?

- Now that your reading of the book is finished, what individual details or general qualities of the book stand out most vividly in your mind?

C. S. Lewis as a young child,
posed in a professional studio portrait and
dressed in traditional infant gown.

This casual Lewis family photograph, circa 1901, shows the Lewis brothers at play with their cousins. R. to L.: Warren Lewis (brother) seated, Leonard Lewis (cousin), C. S. Lewis in white full-length toddler coat, Eileen Lewis (cousin) and Flora Lewis (mother) standing in the background.

Jack and Warnie with their bicycles in August 1908.

C. S. Lewis loved to roam the hills outside Belfast with his brother, Warren. Together, they spent many happy hours walking or bicycling through the rural Irish countryside.

Studio portrait of C. S. Lewis and his father, Albert, in 1918. Albert Lewis was a successful solicitor (lawyer) in the Police Courts of Belfast.

C. S. and Warren Lewis at Annagassan, Ireland, 1949. The two brothers were close friends from childhood and remained so throughout their adult years. Warren (on right with pipe) was a career army officer in the Royal Army Service Corps. After his retirement in 1932, he made his home with his brother, just outside Oxford. During his retirement years, Warren wrote seven books on seventeenth-century France. He also edited the Lewis Family Papers and served as his brother's secretary, assisting him in answering the voluminous correspondence generated in response to C. S. Lewis's popular books and *Mere Christianity* BBC radio broadcasts.

C. S. Lewis at the Kilns, his home outside Oxford.

Headington Quarry Church:
C. S. Lewis's parish church, Holy Trinity
Church (Anglican), where he regularly
attended Sunday worship services.

PRINCE CASPIAN
The Return to Narnia

A Story for Children
by
C. S. LEWIS

IN LOVING MEMORY OF
MY BROTHER
CLIVE STAPLES LEWIS
BORN BELFAST 29TH NOVEMBER 1898
DIED IN THIS PARISH
22ND NOVEMBER 1963
MEN MUST ENDURE THEIR GOING HENCE
WARREN HAMILTON LEWIS
MAJOR ROYAL ARMY SERVICE CORPS
BORN BELFAST 16TH JUNE 1895
DIED IN THIS PARISH
9TH APRIL 1973

Headington Quarry Churchyard:
The gravestone of C. S. Lewis and his
brother, Warren, in the churchyard of Holy
Trinity, Headington Quarry.

First-edition cover of *Prince Caspian*
(1951, Geoffrey Bles publisher).

PART TWO

Caspian Backgrounds

ℰ 16 ℐ

Are the Narnian Stories Allegorical?

Any consideration of the moral and religious vision of the Narnian stories (our topic in the next chapter) depends on an adequate understanding of whether the stories are allegorical. That Lewis wished to steer readers away from regarding the stories as allegories is well attested. But the issue is not as simple as these denials by themselves might suggest. If there are ways in which the stories operate as certain types of allegory do, it is potentially confusing to make a flat denial of the relevance of allegory as a literary form to our reading and interpretation of the Narnian stories.

This chapter is our attempt to disentangle the issues surrounding the question of whether allegory exists in the Narnian stories. We will consider three specific questions: (1) Exactly what did Lewis say and mean when he denied that the Narnian stories are allegories? (2) What are the lessons that readers need to learn from the statements Lewis made on this subject? (3) What are the implications of the ways in which ordinary definitions of allegory fit certain aspects of the Narnian stories?

LEWIS'S DENIALS THAT THE NARNIAN STORIES ARE ALLEGORIES

C. S. Lewis repeatedly denied that the Narnian stories are allegories. To keep the discussion manageable, we have chosen to look at just four of these denials, but in doing so we want to make clear that Lewis made similar comments elsewhere.

We begin with a well-known passage in which Lewis reveals how he composed the Narnian stories—and how he did *not* compose them:

> Some people seem to think that I began by asking myself how I could
> say something about Christianity to children; then fixed on the fairy
> tale as an instrument; then . . . drew up a list of basic Christian truths
> and hammered out "allegories" to embody them. This is all pure
> moonshine. I couldn't write in that way at all. Everything began with
> images. . . . At first there wasn't even anything Christian about them;
> that element pushed itself in of its own accord.

We can note the following things about the statement. First, Lewis rejects
the label *allegories* for the stories. Second, Lewis puts the word *allegories* in
quotation marks, potentially suggesting that he has in view common under-
standings of the word and signaling that other meanings (perhaps legitimate
ones in regard to the Narnian stories) are possible. Third, Lewis is here talking about how he composed the stories, not necessarily how readers might
assimilate them. Finally, although the process of composing the Narnian stories began with no Christian meanings as part of Lewis's creative design,
Christian meanings did emerge as the process unfolded.

In a second quotation taken from a letter written to a class of American
fifth graders, Lewis compares the Narnian books to *Pilgrim's Progress* as a
way of clarifying his imaginative purpose for his children's stories:

> You are mistaken when you think that everything in the books "repre-
> sents" something in this world. Things do that in *The Pilgrim's Progress*
> but I'm not writing in that way. I did not say to myself "Let us repre-
> sent Jesus as He really is in our world by a Lion in Narnia": I said "Let
> us *suppose* that there were a land like Narnia and that the Son of God,
> as He became a Man in our world, became a Lion there, and then
> imagine what would happen." If you think about it, you will see that
> it is quite a different thing.

The most important thing to emerge from this statement is that Lewis did not intend "everything" in the Narnian stories to represent a corresponding reality in our world or (by extension) in Christian experience or theology. This does not necessarily preclude the possibility that *some* things correspond. Second, we note that Lewis was once again commenting on how he composed the stories: he did not *compose* them as allegories. Third, in Lewis's mind the act of *supposing* what the incarnate Christ would be like in an imagined fairy story was "quite a different thing" from allegory.

"In a certain sense, I have never exactly 'made' a story.
With me the process is much more like bird-watching than like either
talking or building. I see pictures. . . . I have no idea whether this is the
usual way of writing stories, still less whether it is the best.
It is the only one I know: images always come first."

C. S. LEWIS, *ON STORIES*

Our third passage is one in which Lewis denies that the Narnian stories are allegorical while defining allegory in a specific way: "By an allegory I mean a composition (whether pictorial or literary) in which immaterial realities are represented by feigned physical objects. . . . If Aslan represented the immaterial Deity in the same way in which Giant Despair represents Despair, he would be an allegorical figure." The type of allegory that Lewis describes here is what literary scholars variously call naive, simple, explicit or continuous allegory. It is clear from this comment that the Narnian stories are certainly not allegorical in the sense that Bunyan's *Pilgrim's Progress* is allegorical (as signaled by Lewis's reference to Giant Despair).

In this same letter Lewis goes on to state unequivocally:

In reality however [Aslan] is an invention giving an imaginary answer to the question, "What might Christ become like if there really were a world like Narnia and He chose to be incarnate and die and rise again in *that* world as He actually has done in ours?" This is not an allegory at all. . . . Allegory and such proposals differ because they mix the real and the unreal in different ways. . . . The Incarnation of Christ in another world is mere supposal: but *granted* the supposition, He would really have been a physical object in that world as He was in Palestine.

In this passage (as well as in other comments he made elsewhere) Lewis is articulating his theory of "supposal," describing not only how he composed his stories but also how he wanted them interpreted. In this regard he markedly distinguishes his "supposals" from allegory, but he nonetheless draws an explicit correspondence between his portrayal of Aslan's actions in the Narnian stories and Christ's actions in the world ("as He was in Palestine").

Our fourth quotation begins to shed light on how we might reconcile the divide between how Lewis understood his stories and how we traditionally understand the literary role of allegory: "The Narnian series is not exactly allegory. I'm not saying 'Let us represent in terms of märchen [German for folk tale or fairy story] the *actual* story of this world.' Rather 'Supposing the Narnian world, let us guess what form the activities of the Second Person or Creator, Redeemer, and Judge might take there.' This, you see, overlaps with allegory but is not quite the same."

This comment by Lewis makes several points apparent. First, even up to the end of his life (this letter was written just months before his death and more than a decade after the first Narnian story was published), Lewis continued to distinguish between his concept of "supposal" and allegory. But as he himself acknowledges here, there is nonetheless genuine overlap between the two literary forms. This means that even if the Narnian stories as a whole are "not exactly allegory," by Lewis's own admission there still must be certain aspects of the stories that bear the characteristics of allegory. In other words, Lewis gives us license to read aspects of his story allegorically—even as he continues to warn against viewing the stories in their entirety as allegory.

IMPLICATIONS FOR READERS OF THE NARNIAN STORIES

With the foregoing statements by Lewis before us, we need to codify the lessons we can learn as readers of the Narnian stories. The most obvious lesson is that Lewis did not wish his stories to be called allegories. Thus, whatever qualifications we might eventually make regarding Lewis's strictures against regarding the stories as allegories, we need to acknowledge that Lewis considered the term *allegory* to be so potentially harmful to a correct understanding of the stories that using this term is ill-advised.

Second, the statements quoted above are in significant part oriented to describing how Lewis composed the stories. He obviously did not write his children's stories with correspondences to theological realities consciously in mind. There is nothing unusual in this: authors throughout history have overwhelmingly affirmed that in the process of composition their decisions are largely intuitive rather than calculated and intellectual. To anticipate what we will say later in this chapter, Lewis's comments about composition need to be balanced by Lewis's statements about what happened after the stories had been composed. It is as though Lewis's nonallegorical intentions while composing freed him up to be true to the narrative qualities of his fairy tale of adventure and fantasy, unencumbered by thoughts of the religious meaning of his story.

It is also helpful to speculate as to why Lewis disliked calling the Narnian stories allegorical. We can infer that Lewis feared that allegorical interpretation runs an inherent risk of being reductionistic. Lewis implied that allegorical readings often shortchange the imaginative nature of a good story by too quickly moving from creative image to abstraction (or meaning).

In an essay on Bunyan's *Pilgrim's Progress* Lewis disapproves of reading an allegorical story in such a way that, "having grasped what an image . . . 'means,' we [throw] the image away" and concentrate on what "it represents." That is a flawed way of reading because it "leads you continually out of the book back into the conception you started from and would have had without reading it." Of course one does not *need* to read allegory in this way, and in fact Lewis immediately opens the door to reading allegory in what he calls the "right" way—by advising that one should move "always into the book," resisting the impulse to shift away from the image and instead allowing the image to "[enrich] the concept." And then Lewis adds the statement "That is what allegory is for," implying his endorsement of the form of allegory as having literary value in principle.

We can summarize Lewis's views on this subject by saying that he saw an inherent danger that readers will reduce stories to a conceptual and abstract level if they interpret them allegorically, though it is possible to read allegorically without succumbing to this tendency. Lewis underscores this point when he writes, "Let the pictures tell you their own moral."

"My view would be that a good myth (i.e., a story out of which ever varying meanings will grow for different readers and in different ages) is a higher thing than an allegory (into which one meaning has been put). Into an allegory a man can put only what he already knows: in a myth he puts what he does not yet know and could not come to know in any other way."

C. S. LEWIS, *COLLECTED LETTERS*

In addition to fearing reductionism Lewis was also concerned about the practice some readers of his Narnian stories had of finding allegorical meanings where he did not intend them and where they did not exist. He cautioned, "As we know, almost anything can be read into any book if you are determined enough. This will be especially impressed on anyone who has written fantastic fiction. He will find reviewers, both favourable and hostile, reading into his stories all manner of allegorical meanings which he never intended. . . . Apparently it is impossible for the wit of man to devise a narrative in which the wit of some other man cannot, and with some plausibility, find a hidden sense."

It is obvious that Lewis desired most of all that his children's fiction would be enjoyed as stories—"received," in the literary sense, and not simply "used" didactically. In this context, to *receive* a story means to fully experience it by imaginatively entering into the narrative much as a young child might do. In contrast, to *use* a story in the didactic sense is to focus primarily upon information to be extracted and analyzed—much as one might approach a textbook. This is not to say that meaning is absent when one receives a story but rather that meaning is enhanced because we encounter it not only with our intellect but also with our heart. (Lewis's helpful comments on the difference between receiving a work of art and using it can be found in *An Experiment in Criticism*.) For example, in chapter ten of *Prince Caspian,* when we enter imaginatively into the account of the reunion between Lucy and Aslan—feeling along with Lucy her heartfelt joy as she responds to the Great Lion's tender welcome—we begin to experience a sense of what divine love entails. Or to put it another way, in this scene we not only learn about the love of God but also, as a result of the creative power of story, doctrinal teachings on divine love begin to come alive for us as readers.

"The figure of Aslan ... tells us more of how Lewis understood the nature of God than anything else he wrote. It has all the hidden power and majesty and awesomeness which Lewis associated with God, but also the glory and the tenderness and even the humour which he believed belonged to him, so that children could run up to him and throw their arms round him and kiss him. . . . It is 'mere Christianity.'"

DOM BEDE GRIFFITHS, *CANADIAN CSL JOURNAL*

The lessons we can learn from Lewis's disavowals that the Narnian stories are allegories can be summarized as follows: (1) We need to acknowledge that popular conceptions of allegory make that word a risky term to use with the Narnian stories. (2) We need to read with an awareness that the stories were not composed as allegories. (3) The first item on our agenda as readers of the stories is to assimilate the material as an imaginative construct and never to allow abstract conceptual meanings to become a substitute for the images of the story (broadly defined to include events, characters and settings). (4) We need to be on our guard against seeing religious meanings where they do not exist.

ALLEGORICAL DIMENSIONS OF THE NARNIAN STORIES

We have noted that Lewis's strictures against viewing his stories as allegories seem to flow first and foremost from his role as author of the stories. But other statements made by Lewis, sometimes apparently in his role as reader or critic of his stories, show the issues to be more complex than they at first appear. Two and a half years before his death, for example, Lewis wrote to a young girl that, if she would read *The Lion, the Witch and the Wardrobe,* "I think that you will probably see that there is deeper meaning behind it. The whole Narnian story is about Christ." And, as noted earlier in this chapter, Lewis wrote elsewhere that although initially "there wasn't even anything Christian about [the stories]," later the Christian "element pushed itself in of its own accord." This shows that Lewis saw much more in his stories than simply the imaginative pictures with which they began.

Do these statements by Lewis imply an allegorical level of meaning in the Narnian stories? We can answer that question by taking an excursion into allegory as a literary form. A good starting point is Lewis himself, since he is a major authority on allegory. Lewis wrote a landmark book on medieval allegory, entitled *The Allegory of Love: A Study in Medieval Tradition,* that to this day is considered a classic of literary scholarship. Furthermore one of the two English authors on whom Lewis wrote the greatest quantity of literary criticism was Edmund Spenser, and a great deal of that commentary discusses the allegorical features of *The Faerie Queene.* In all of this literary commentary Lewis emerges as one who enjoyed and valued allegory as a literary form.

One of Lewis's most provocative statements in *The Allegory of Love* is that "every metaphor is an allegory in little." This is a highly novel sentiment, showing that Lewis was capable of finding allegory in an unlikely place. How can a metaphor be viewed as an allegory? Upon reflection, we can see a basis for the claim: the essential method of both metaphor and allegory is double meaning. The etymology of the word *allegory* shows that it is based on the two concepts of "speaking" and "other," yielding the root "to speak so as to imply something other." Similarly the word *metaphor* is based on the Greek "to carry over." Both metaphor and allegory have two levels of meaning, with a correspondence between them.

The kind of continuous or simple allegory that Lewis apparently had in mind when he denied that the Narnian stories are allegories is not the only kind of allegory that exists. In the mid-twentieth century, literary critic Northrop Frye gave the literary world a view of allegory that was widely accepted by scholars who were familiar with it. Instead of viewing works of literature as being either allegorical or nonallegorical, Frye proposed the idea of an allegorical continuum that allows us to gauge the degree to which or way in which a work is allegorical.

At one end of the allegorical continuum we find what Frye called explicit and continuous allegories, in which the details of a story consistently have a second meaning. Next we have texts "with a large and insistent doctrinal interest, in which the internal fictions are exempla, like the epics of Milton." "In the exact center" we find works such as Shakespeare's plays in which the meanings have been completely embodied in the details of the story, so that we pay equal attention to the details of the text and the meanings embodied in it. At the far end of the continuum the details in the text begin "to recede from example and precept" and approximate journalistic reportage.

A Spenser scholar named Graham Hough popularized Frye's paradigm for Spenser studies. Hough spoke of the two main impulses in literature as "literature in which theme is dominant, and literature in which image is dominant." Hough proposed the word *incarnation* to denote works in the center of the continuum—literature "in which theme and image seem equally balanced."

The general drift of this framework is to allow us to identify degrees to which a work is allegorical. The more a work moves toward the explicit and continuous end of the continuum, the more inclined we are to call the work as a whole allegorical. But even if we stop short of that label for an entire work, we can speak of allegorical elements or episodes in a story.

A concomitant of Frye's and Hough's paradigm is the conclusion that literature as a whole, as well as literary criticism as a whole, has an incipient allegorical cast to it. Thus Hough claims that "allegory in its broadest possible sense is a pervasive element in all literature." In the same vein Frye claimed that "all commentary is allegorical interpretation, an attaching of ideas to the structure of poetic imagery. The instant that any critic permits himself to make a genuine comment about a poem (e.g., 'In *Hamlet* Shakespeare appears to be portraying the tragedy of irresolution') he has begun to allegorize." As a preliminary application to the Narnian stories, the religious themes that Lewis attached to each of the seven Narnian stories (see boxed item) are an obvious example of assigning what some literary critics would call an allegorical religious meaning to the action. We might note in passing, moreover, that the religious meanings that Lewis attaches to the individual stories are more specific than most readers would come up with on their own.

To summarize, the essential method of allegory is that some details in a story stand for something in addition to themselves, without ceasing to have a literal or concrete existence as details in a story. Jesus' parables are good examples. With the parable of the soils, for example, Jesus provided a corresponding "other" meaning to every detail in the story except the sower (Mt 13:1-9, 18-23). There is even a sense in which all composers of allegory engage in an act of what Lewis called supposal: in the parable of the soils, Jesus *supposed* that the proclamation of the gospel to various types of hearers is like a farmer sowing seeds in various types of soil.

Lewis himself, in his commentary on Spenser's allegorical technique in *The Faerie Queene,* provides an additional helpful framework by which to understand his own technique in the Narnian stories. In each book of *The*

"The whole Narnian story is about Christ. That is to say, I asked myself 'Supposing there really were a world like Narnia, and supposing it had (like our world) gone wrong, and supposing Christ wanted to go into that world and save it (as He did ours) what might have happened?"

"The stories are my answer. . . . The whole series works out like this:

The Magician's Nephew *tells the creation and how evil entered Narnia.*

The Lion etc—*the Crucifixion and Resurrection*

Prince Caspian—*restoration of the true religion after a corruption*

The Horse and his Boy—*the calling and conversion of a heathen.*

The Voyage of the Dawn Treader—*the spiritual life (specially in Reepicheep)*

The Silver Chair—*the continued war against the powers of darkness*

The Last Battle—*the coming of Antichrist (the Ape). The end of the world, and the Last Judgement"*

C. S. LEWIS, *COLLECTED LETTERS*

Faerie Queene, theorized Lewis, there is "an allegorical core" in which we find the message of a given book laid out to view in explicit, continuous allegory, "disentangled from the complex adventures" found elsewhere in the book. Second, the overall plot of the individual books represents "the main allegorical story of the book." Beyond that we find episodes of adventure and fantasy that are either loosely allegorical or "not allegorical at all." We might note in passing that the range that Lewis outlines corresponds with the stages on the allegorical continuum proposed by Frye and Hough.

What we find in the Narnian stories is approximately what Lewis identifies in Spenser's *Faerie Queene,* a work that exerted a strong and steady influence on the Narnian stories. At least half the story material in all the Narnian books consists of fairy-tale adventure with no overt religious meanings. Usually we do not start thinking of religious meanings until around halfway through the books. To find religious meanings in this strictly narrative material is to allegorize the text—to attach corresponding meanings to the details in a text that was not intended by the author to yield such meanings. We should note in passing, therefore, a crucial difference between allegorizing a text and interpreting an allegorical text. In the latter case the author *did* intend the details to have a corresponding "other" meaning.

Second, each of the Narnian stories has an overall allegorical action in which the main story line embodies an intended religious theme (see box on page 103 for Lewis's own identifications). We might actually find multiple allegorical actions. Thus if the overall plot of *Prince Caspian* pictures "the restoration of the true religion after a corruption" (Lewis's formula), it equally embodies such themes as the life of Christian discipleship (including obedience, trust, faith, devotion and so on) and the triumph of Aslan/Christ over the forces of evil.

Third, the Narnian stories also have passages where we find repeated and continuous tie-ins between characters and events in the story and Christian experience. For example, chapters fourteen and fifteen of *The Lion, the Witch and the Wardrobe* are the "allegorical core" of that book as a whole—the place where the overall theme of Christ's "Crucifixion and Resurrection" (Lewis's own formula) is embodied in specific detail. As we read these chapters, numerous details correspond to events in the Passion and Resurrection stories in the Gospels. There is nothing as explicit as that in *Prince Caspian,* but there are numerous points at which we are aware as we read that what is actually being portrayed is how believers in Christ live in relation to him. For example, the love and reverence that the children feel toward Aslan, the Lion's instruction to Lucy to follow him no matter how others respond, and Trumpkin's coming to believe in the existence of Aslan (his conversion) all correspond to familiar aspects of the Christian life. We cannot suppress such double meanings if we tried.

The allegorical nature of the Narnian stories stands highlighted if we place those stories of Aslan beside the fable of Androcles and the lion. The story of the friendly lion in the fable shows us what a nonallegorical story looks like. Even though the fable itself has a moral ("Gratitude is the sign of noble souls"), there are no corresponding "other" meanings to the figure of the lion or the person of the slave—they do not represent anything other than themselves as characters in the story. But in the Narnian stories we are regularly reminded of features of the Christian life as embodied in the characters and events in the stories, and the Great Lion Aslan clearly represents Christ.

THE CRUX

Putting all of the foregoing together, it is obvious that the question of allegory in the Narnian stories is a great deal more complicated than we might expect from the customary denial by Lewis scholars that the stories are allegories. On the one hand, we find a large body of data that would dissuade us from describing the Narnian stories as allegories. On the other hand, we find that the stories display many of the usual features of allegorical literature. The chief of these is the technique of double meanings whereby details in the text are intended to elicit an additional meaning that ties into a corresponding "other" story. The authors of this book divide on the question of how to deal with the conflicting data.

One of us believes (as Lewis clearly asserted) that to use the term *allegory* for the Narnian stories poses sufficient potential hazards as not to be worth the risk. Lewis himself did not want us to understand the stories as traditional allegories. Nor did he intentionally compose them as allegories. Furthermore the literary form of allegory is laden with the inherent pitfall of being reductionistic. The mere label may lead readers into inferior ways of reading the stories, chiefly by not allowing the narrative qualities of the stories to come alive in their imaginations but also by imposing allegorical meanings where they do not exist. Nonetheless it must be acknowledged that even though the Narnian books, in their entirety, should not be understood as allegories, there are still allegorical elements to be found within the stories. And the best approach to understanding the religious significance of these allegorical elements is to allow the story itself to signal the Christian meaning, so that we as readers receive it experientially and imaginatively from *within* the narrative (rather than impose it upon the text from the outside).

The other one of us believes that (to use the proverbial saying) if a bird quacks like a duck, waddles like a duck and swims like a duck, it *is* a duck. It is well established that Lewis intended us to draw correspondences between Aslan and Christ, between the main plot line of the individual books and a Christian theme, and between numerous details in the stories and aspects of the Christian life. In any other circumstance we would call such elements in a story allegorical. Furthermore it is confusing to readers to be told that the stories are not allegories but then expect them to perform the usual interpretive activities that allegory entails, chiefly drawing correspondences between details in the text and Christian experience and theology.

However, this disagreement about labeling should not be allowed to obscure the large amount of agreement that exists between the two viewpoints. What is *not* open to dispute, in the estimate of the authors of this book, is that we must give full imaginative force to the first or literal story line, that we must insist on a plausible warrant in the text before we make religious connections with details in the text, that we must respect Lewis's comments about how he composed the Narnian stories and that Lewis himself distrusted the term *allegory* as a label for his stories.

ℰ 17 ℐ

The Christian Vision of Prince Caspian

Some of the most helpful commentary on the religious vision of the Narnian chronicles appears in a letter C. S. Lewis wrote two and a half years before his death. In explaining his intended link between Aslan and Christ, Lewis wrote, "The whole Narnian story is about Christ." This unequivocal assertion by Lewis is key to understanding his religious purpose for each one of the Chronicles of Narnia. Indeed, as Lewis explains elsewhere, although he did not begin writing with the intention of embodying Christian truths in his stories, the character of Aslan "just insisted on behaving in His own way . . . and the whole series became Christian."

As we noted in the last chapter, in addition to making these comments on the whole Narnian series, Lewis also offered an explanation of the religious meaning of the overall action in *Prince Caspian*. Writing to answer the questions of a young girl, Lewis explained that the religious theme of *Prince Caspian* is the "restoration of the true religion after corruption." This statement is, of course, a very general formulation of the religious theme of *Prince Caspian,* but it is also the best starting point if we wish to read *Prince Caspian* with C. S. Lewis, as it were.

The true religion is what prevailed in Old Narnia, in the days when Aslan was known and loved and obeyed by his followers. (In the same way we understand that being a Christian involves loving and submitting to Christ and following him.) The Narnians living in King Miraz's kingdom who still remember the true religion and continue to loyally believe in Aslan are reminders of the biblical archetype of the faithful remnant of adherents to the faith—those who survive apostasy and persecution in order to reestablish true religion in the end.

And what about the loss of the true religion that Miraz's regime promotes? It is a horror story in which the main images are dehumanization, bondage, tyranny, terror to the good accompanied by elevation of evil, and the desecration of nature. Most of all, the loss of the true religion creates a climate where there is a deep hatred of Aslan and all he represents.

Within this generalized framework of the restoration of true religion, we can discern a moral dimension and multiple theological themes. The moral vision concerns human behavior toward fellow creatures. On the theological side, five main ideas are embodied in the story: (1) the conflict between good and evil in the universe, (2) providence, (3) faith, (4) discipleship and

(5) the presence and work of Christ/Aslan in the world. (The identification of Aslan with Christ is confirmed by the story of his atoning death and resurrection in *The Lion, the Witch and the Wardrobe* as well as by statements made by Lewis such as the one quoted earlier.)

"THE MIRROR OF HONOR": THE MORAL VISION

The moral vision of any work of literature is easy to determine. It consists of the virtues that a work offers for approval and the vices that it holds up for disapproval. Because the Narnian chronicles are stories of characters in action, they necessarily embody a moral vision consisting of moral examples. These examples, in turn, fall into the two categories of (1) positive behavior held up for emulation and (2) negative behavior designed to elicit a reader's rejection.

Additionally the moral vision of fantasy inclines overwhelmingly not to be subtle or ambiguous but instead to be clear-cut. In fact this is one of the strengths of fantasy as a genre. The ethics of fantasy, G. K. Chesterton wrote in an essay titled "The Ethics of Elfland," belong to "the sunny country of common sense." In other words, whenever we encounter individuals in a fantasy story, it is usually quickly evident—most often by their behavior—whether or not we are to approve of them or perceive them as villains.

An easy example of this distinction can be found by looking at the followers of Caspian in comparison to the followers of Miraz. When the Old Narnians (such as Trufflehunter the Badger, the Dwarf Trumpkin and Reepicheep the valiant Mouse) first encounter Caspian, they barely know him, and yet they are willing to sacrifice everything for the values he represents. In response Caspian feels a responsibility for these newfound subjects and does his best to fulfill his duty toward them and all of Aslan's Narnia. These noble actions of Caspian and his followers reflect personal courage and self-sacrifice.

In contrast the false usurper King Miraz has been treacherously disloyal to his brother (the rightful king, whom he has slain in order to acquire his throne). He extends that betrayal when he seeks to murder his innocent nephew Caspian as well. Not surprisingly, Miraz's closest advisers are, in

———————————————————— ⌒◞◟ ————————————————————

"This Rule of Right and Wrong, or Law of Human Nature, . . . must somehow or other be a real thing—a thing that is really there, not made up by ourselves. And yet it is not a fact in the ordinary sense, in the same way as our actual behaviour is a fact. It begins to look as if we shall have to admit that there is more than one kind of reality; that, in this particular case, there is something above and beyond the ordinary facts of men's behaviour, and yet quite definitely real—a real law, which none of us made, but which we find pressing on us."

C. S. LEWIS, *MERE CHRISTIANITY*

---

turn, disloyal to him. Though they have been with Miraz for many years and have benefited from his position of power, they do not feel any bond of obligation and are ready to betray the King the moment it is to their advantage. Thus their actions illustrate the selfishness and evil intentions that arise when one lives only for oneself.

A general summary of the moral virtues of the Narnian stories, including *Prince Caspian,* would include this list: courage, loyalty, honesty, generosity, hospitality, self-sacrifice, selflessness and seeking the good of others. The moral vices of the Narnian stories are found in such destructive elements as selfishness, betrayal, deceitfulness, tyranny and cruelty. Beyond these specific virtues and vices, the Narnian stories belong to that category of literature in which we experience good and evil as moral realities and principles in themselves. Characters in *Prince Caspian* are ultimately either good or evil depending upon whether they give their allegiance to Aslan or not. The simplicity of this moral scheme should not be allowed to obscure how central it is to the stories nor its profundity.

"OLD NARNIA IN DANGER": THE COSMIC BATTLE BETWEEN GOOD AND EVIL

Balancing the moral vision of the Narnian stories is the theological vision. If we take a wide-angle view of the Narnian stories, the primary theological reality is the same as it is in the Bible—the cosmic, all-encompassing conflict between good and evil. We are nearly always aware of this great spiritual battle for the supremacy of the world as we read the Narnian stories. This is partly because Lewis was writing fairy stories, where the omnipresent threat of evil is the mainspring of the plot.

In *Prince Caspian* the leaders in the cosmic spiritual battle are Aslan and Miraz. However, this story does not set the two of them in opposition in the same way that there is ongoing conflict between Aslan and the White Witch in *The Lion, the Witch and the Wardrobe.* Instead in *Prince Caspian* the battle is waged between the followers of Aslan and the followers of Miraz. As a result, at key points the struggle is not epic but instead unfolds on an inner stage of the individual human soul. Indeed virtually all the characters in *Prince Caspian* are required to make a choice between Aslan and Miraz. This narrative conflict is ultimately resolved by the triumph of the Great Lion over various figures and forces of evil—a demonstration of the power and authority gained by Aslan through his sacrificial death on the Stone Table in *The Lion, the Witch and the Wardrobe* (this victorious might is evocative of the theological atonement tradition known as *Christus Victor*).

"There is no neutral ground in the universe: every square inch, every split second, is claimed by God and counterclaimed by Satan."

C. S. LEWIS, *CHRISTIAN REFLECTIONS*

An example of Aslan's filling this redemptive role can be found toward the end of *Prince Caspian* when the Great Lion majestically sweeps through the countryside, releasing both the natural world and the inhabitants of Narnia from the bondage they have suffered (a scene reminiscent of J. R. R. Tolkien's "scouring of the shire" at the end of *The Lord of the Rings*). The coming enthronement of Caspian as rightful king will not be enough to redeem the evil that has been perpetrated by the prior regime. In order for true renewal to occur Narnia needs more than simply a change of leadership—the land itself and its inhabitants need deep and genuine healing. However, though this redemptive grace is offered by Aslan to all, only those Telmarines who are willing for a change of heart to take place within them will remain. The others, those who refuse to trust and obey Aslan, will leave Narnia and be returned to their ancestral home on earth.

"ASLAN LED THEM": PROVIDENCE

When Prince Caspian blows Susan's horn to summon help in the battle to win back Old Narnia, neither he nor his adviser Doctor Cornelius knows what form the assistance will take. Furthermore, when the four Pevensie children arrive in Narnia, they haven't a clue as to what is happening to them. Only when Trumpkin provides the background behind the children's arrival in Narnia does a goal emerge, namely the need to reach Aslan's How and join forces with Prince Caspian.

But even when the five start out on a two-day journey to reach that goal, they have no clear-cut plan for how to get there. In fact, throughout their trek to reach Caspian's army, their path is frequently determined by unforeseen circumstances that override their own decisions. For example, they initially set out for the Fords of Beruna but have to reverse and travel back up the gorge to escape the danger posed by Miraz's pursuing sentries. What the party lacks is guidance on their journey. Because they are left to their own designs, the journey is a litany of failures from which the group finally needs to be rescued.

An important aspect of the Christian doctrine of providence is that it involves God's guidance of individuals and events to achieve his purposes in the world and to care for his people. In *Prince Caspian,* after a series of meanderings and wrong decisions on the part of the five travelers, Aslan appears and guides the party on the right path. The story records a series of details regarding how Aslan led the group—along the top of precipices, down a deep gorge, across a stream, up a steep path, up another steep path, up the face of more precipices, up a gentle slope and finally within view of the hill of the Stone Table. At the narrative level this action is the archetypal perilous journey in which heroes are aided by a supernatural force. But as elsewhere in the Narnian stories, the romance motifs have a significance beyond the literary level. The guidance provided by Aslan on the perilous journey is a picture of divine providence.

Providential guidance in *Prince Caspian* does not rely on the initiation of the person who receives the guidance. It depends instead on a character's willingness to be guided. For example, when the four Pevensie children are first "pulled" into Narnia by Susan's enchanted Horn, this occurrence does not occur in response to any intentional act on their part. But once in Narnia, the children need to choose whether they will help Caspian and his beleaguered army. Thus, though divine guidance is not given as a reward for human actions, the efficacy of this help can be thwarted if an individual chooses to ignore providential guidance once it is offered. An example of this can be found in the initial refusal of Peter, Edmund and Susan to acknowledge Aslan's presence when he first appears to guide them to Caspian's camp. Because of their inability to receive the help offered, they make decisions that result in nearly disastrous complications for the success of their mission.

"WHO BELIEVES IN ASLAN NOWADAYS?": FAITH

Lewis devotes even more attention to the experience of faith—faith in the supernatural generally and in Aslan (or Christ) specifically. The key action is the pattern of individuals gradually coming to see and thereby acknowledge the presence of Aslan. As the journey unfolds, first Lucy and then each of the other three children (Edmund, Peter and Susan) gradually comes to see and thereby acknowledge Aslan's presence. Eventually even the skeptic Trumpkin will renounce his earlier doubts about the existence of the Great Lion.

There are two possible ways of viewing these pictures of faith in Aslan/ Christ. On the face of it, the story appears to directly link seeing Aslan with believing in him. Viewed from this angle, characters come to believe in Aslan only as they are given evidence of his presence. But Peter Schakel maintains that Lewis actually reverses the adage that seeing is believing, giving us instead an image of how believing is seeing. Or as Schakel explains, in *Prince Caspian* (as in other of Lewis's stories), "those who believe are able to see; those who do not believe cannot see." In other words, unless Lucy had already truly believed in Aslan, she would not have been able to see him. Some readers may find it helpful to consider this in the context of a statement by Anselm, eleventh-century archbishop of Canterbury, who declared: "For I do not seek to understand in order to believe but I believe in order to understand. For I believe even this: that I shall not understand unless I believe." In other words, if seeing in this context is equated with understanding, then for the Pevensie children to truly "see" (or understand) Aslan, they must first believe. Hence faith necessarily precedes understanding (or seeing). But Lewis's own commitment to apologetics—to grounding belief in good reasons—is also well attested, and a close look at chapter eleven of *Prince Caspian* will show that either interpretation is plausible.

"[In life] . . . *as in the New Testament, the conflict is not between faith and reason, but between faith and sight. . . . Our faith in Christ wavers not so much when real arguments come against it as when it looks improbable.*"

C. S. LEWIS, "RELIGION: REALITY OR SUBSTITUTE?"

As always, Lucy is the character who evidences the most spiritual depth and sensitivity in the story. This motif begins in chapter ten when Lucy hears her voice called in the middle of the night and enters the forest. In the middle of this enchanted woods Lucy is joyfully reunited with Aslan. But it is also in this scene that Lucy receives Aslan's command to rouse her fellow travelers to follow him, no matter what it costs her personally. Her happiness at seeing Aslan is accordingly tempered by her reluctance to obey his difficult command. But obey him she does, and in spite of her misgivings she awakens the others and tells them what they must do.

Aslan's caution to Lucy that the others would not see him "at first," but perhaps "later on, it depends," proves to be true as her siblings initially do not see Aslan. But, one by one, they do gradually come to see him. Eventually even Trumpkin is forced to acknowledge the existence of Aslan—and as such he becomes a "convert." However, Edmund, Peter and Susan do not need to be converted to belief in Aslan. They already believe (in the abstract), having known Aslan well during their earlier days in Narnia. But they need to make a confession of their belief in the existential present as a prerequisite to seeing Aslan now. This interplay between believing and seeing is actually a literary portrayal of the dynamics of belief in Christ and the supernatural.

"There must perhaps always be just enough lack of demonstrative certainty to make free choice possible: for what could we do but accept if the faith were like the multiplication table?"

C. S. LEWIS; LETTER TO SHELDON VANAUKEN

Juxtaposed against the Pevensie children's difficulty in seeing Aslan is the instant recognition that comes to the aged Nurse when she first sets eyes on the Great Lion. After a lifetime of faithful waiting, her unwavering belief in Aslan is rewarded at last. Though all she had known of Aslan came solely from the old stories (tales that she, in turn, had passed along to Caspian as a child), there is no fear in her first encounter with the Lion. Her joyful words—"I knew it was true. I've been waiting for this all my life"—eloquently convey her complete trust and devotion.

FINDING ASLAN BIGGER: DISCIPLESHIP

Prince Caspian also embodies pictures of Christian discipleship. The prime example is Lucy, but all those who claim allegiance to Aslan learn important lessons about following him during the course of this story. What does it mean to follow Aslan? First and foremost it means loving him and wanting to be with him. Lucy is the great example of this devotion, especially in the reunion scene in the woods in chapter ten. When Lucy sees the Great Lion, she rushes to him, kisses him and throws her arms around his neck. Her joyful response to being in Aslan's presence is wholehearted and without reserve.

The next thing we learn in this scene is that Aslan seems bigger to Lucy than she remembered his being (from the time when she was last in Narnia). Aslan explains that this is not because he is actually bigger but because Lucy herself has grown. Thus we understand that to be a disciple means experiencing that Christ (Aslan) is greater than we first realized and ever more sufficient as life unfolds. Elsewhere Lewis comments on how our perception of God changes as our relationship with him grows by declaring that God "must constantly work as the iconoclast. Every idea of Him we form, He must in mercy shatter. The most blessed result of prayer would be to rise thinking 'But I never knew before, I never dreamed.' "

But the story goes beyond this. Immediately after the scene just referenced, Lucy is rebuked by Aslan for not having the courage to leave the others and follow him when she first had seen him. Even though Lucy did try to persuade her companions to follow Aslan up the gorge instead of down it, when they refused to believe her, she abandoned Aslan's direction and submitted to the wishes of the others. Aslan makes it clear to Lucy that her weakness in not following him, no matter what it cost her, was a failure on her part. Subsequently Lucy acts upon this lesson when she courageously rouses a reluctant party and convinces them to follow the leading of Aslan. Aslan's influence is evident in other aspects of Lucy's actions as well. Even though she was smarting from the taunting of Susan, Lucy forgot her own impulse to retaliate "when she fixed her eyes on Aslan." It is obvious that discipleship in this story is conceived as individual obedience to Christ—no matter what others around us may think or do.

"We might think that God wanted simply obedience to a set of rules: whereas He really wants people of a particular sort."

C. S. LEWIS, *MERE CHRISTIANITY*

"THE RETURN OF THE LION": ASLAN AS CHRIST

The final dimension of the religious vision of *Prince Caspian* is the dominant one, namely the portrayal of Aslan as an implied picture of the nature and work of Christ in the world. Lewis's own testimony about his composition of the Narnian chronicles goes like this: "At first I had very little idea how the story would go. But then suddenly Aslan came bounding into it. . . . Once he was there He pulled the whole story together." It is obvious that Aslan pulled together not only the narrative but also the religious vision. Without the equation of Aslan as Christ, the Narnian stories do not move beyond a moral vision of virtues and vices and a generalized picture of the cosmic conflict between good and evil that we might find in any other fantasy story. But in making the equation of Aslan with Christ, we should also keep in mind that our understanding of Aslan as a Christ figure is best informed by the narrative itself.

What is Aslan like? That is the primary theological question of *Prince Caspian*. To begin, Aslan (Christ) is the object of devotion on the part of those who love him. As already noted, the key scene in which we see this is Lucy's reunion with Aslan in the nighttime scene set in the woods. The moment is repeated when the other three children are reunited with Aslan after having finally seen him, and we read that "they felt as glad as anyone can who feels afraid, and as afraid as anyone can who feels glad." A truly charming moment is the passing comment that during the all-night celebration Lucy was "sitting close to Aslan and divinely comfortable."

Aslan (that is, Christ) is also the one who elicits reverence. When the High King Peter stands before Aslan, he drops to one knee. A few moments later, when Aslan roars, the sound (which Lewis describes as being deep and resounding like a swelling note from a pipe organ) fills the air and causes Miraz's soldiers to blanch in fear. However, Aslan's followers, though filled with respect for his great might, are not in fear of him. Rather they know the Great Lion as their protector as well as their rightful sovereign. Indeed it is only Aslan's presence that allows Lucy and Susan to feel safe with the wild Bacchus and his exuberant friends.

"To love and admire anything outside yourself is to take one step away
from utter spiritual ruin; though we shall not be well so long as we love
and admire anything more than we love and admire God."

C. S. LEWIS, *MERE CHRISTIANITY*

Part of this reverence is the implicit acknowledgment of those who follow Aslan that he is their rightful judge and the one who must forgive them of misdeeds. Lucy says "I'm sorry" to Aslan for her judgmental attitude toward her siblings. Peter says the same thing when he encounters Aslan face to face and is suddenly aware of his failings. Edmund receives the commendation "Well done," while Susan receives Aslan's rebuke over the way in which she had listened to her fears in regard to her belligerence to Lucy (when Lucy virtually forced the group to follow Aslan's leading on the journey).

Aslan as deity is also all knowing, as seen in his ability to lead the Pevensies on the path to Aslan's How as well as in his knowledge of how future events will turn out. And of course Aslan-as-Christ is sovereign and all-powerful. The power of Aslan is underscored by the fact that even when he is physically absent his name and desires still permeate and inform the actions of his followers.

If he is all-powerful, we might pause to ask, why has Narnia fallen into such corruption and unbelief? For the same reasons that our own once-perfect earth became corrupted—to the extent that at some times, in some places, "the whole world lies in the power of the evil one" (1 Jn 5:19). Narnia, too, is subject to evil. However, despite the sad state of Old Narnia when the story opens, Aslan is ultimately sovereign.

"Why is God landing in this enemy-occupied world in disguise? . . . Why is He not landing in force, invading it? Is it that He is not strong enough? Well, Christians think He is going to land in force; we do not know when. But we can guess why He is delaying. He wants to give us the chance of joining His side freely."

C. S. LEWIS, *MERE CHRISTIANITY*

We see Aslan's divine power most fully in the scene in which he leads a frolicking group on a victory procession that transforms the perverted new Narnia back into its original and natural state (chapter fourteen). As leader of this celebratory march, the Great Lion frees both the land of Narnia and its inhabitants from enslavement to all manner of illness and corruption. It is in effect an extended miracle story, reminiscent of miracle stories in the Bible. And of course the miracles continue in the final chapter of *Prince Caspian*, where "Aslan makes a door in the air," with accompanying wonders. The victory procession that Aslan leads while the battle with the followers of Miraz is being waged has a precursor in Aslan's "Romp" back in chapter eleven. The only way to make sense of the bacchanal in that chapter is to interpret it as evidence that Christ can redeem even the wildest impulses of humanity and creation.

If Aslan-as-Christ has the attributes and powers noted above, it goes without saying that he is the supreme being whom all creatures need either to accept or reject as Lord. And in this regard the motif from ancient literature known as *the divine-human encounter* makes notable appearances in *Prince Caspian*. The Pevensie children all express reverential devotion when

Religious Themes in Prince Caspian: *Critical Views*

Whereas the religious content of The Lion, the Witch and the Wardrobe *is unmistakably the story of Christ's atoning death and resurrection, the story that Lewis tells in* Prince Caspian *is less clear-cut and more open to a range of religious interpretations. Below is a summary of what some of the critics surveyed in chapter nineteen ("The Critics Comment on* Prince Caspian*") have seen as the religious import of the story.*

- *The transcendence of God, who exists outside ordinary time* (David C. Downing)
- *Learning valor and righteousness from wise mentors* (Bruce L. Edwards)
- *The psychological problems involved in believing the Christian faith* (Paul F. Ford)
- *The character of Aslan/Christ; the conflict between good and evil; the growth of a soul in knowledge of Jesus* (Jacqueline Foulon)
- *Faith in an age of doubt* (Evan K. Gibson)
- *Testing of faith in Aslan/Christ; the heroism of Lucy's belief and obedience* (Donald E. Glover)
- *The portrayal of Lucy as Christian mystic* (Richard Johnston)
- *The harmonizing of Christianity and paganism* (Gareth Knight)
- *Joy in the context of self-control* (Doris T. Myers)
- *The characters' struggling with issues of faith and doubt in regard to Old Narnia as a picture of how people wrestle with the claims of Christianity in our world* (Jonathan Rogers)
- *Belief versus unbelief, and the triumph of faith* (Peter J. Schakel)

they encounter Aslan. Though the skeptic Dwarf Trumpkin expresses early doubts about the existence of the Great Lion, he is brought to a conversion by Aslan himself in chapter eleven. Prince Caspian, the rightful human sovereign of Narnia, kneels and kisses the Lion's paw when he first meets Aslan in chapter fifteen. When the Telmarines are given the choice to remain in Narnia under conditions laid down by Aslan or return to Telmar, some accept the invitation to remain, while others do not.

Even though *Prince Caspian* lacks the overtly theological content of the atoning death and resurrection of Aslan in *The Lion, the Witch and the Wardrobe,* it turns out to express an extended Christian vision. The characterization and actions of Aslan are the key to this religious vision.

℮ 18 ℈

Contemporary Reviews of Prince Caspian

The summaries of contemporary reviews that we offer in this chapter offer a glimpse into how *Prince Caspian* was viewed by readers and reviewers immediately upon its release in 1951. After the initial success of *The Lion, the Witch and the Wardrobe,* reviewers were increasingly enthusiastic about the new story, but fantasy was still an emerging genre for children. Lewis biographer George Sayer has noted that "at the time the books appeared, the real-life children's story was in fashion. It was commonly believed then that stories should help children to understand and relate to real life, that they should not encourage them to indulge in fantasies, and that fairy stories, if for any children at all, should only be for the very young."

It is interesting to note that, in terms of the recommended reading levels, there was a tendency to identify *Prince Caspian* as being most suitable for children older than the average age of children who read this story today. We have found that this book is usually read around the third or fourth grade (or even earlier, if read aloud to the child by an adult).

In the following excerpts we have primarily let the reviewers speak for themselves. It is easy to observe the common threads that run throughout the reviews. These commonalities include:

- conspicuous linking of the story to *The Lion, the Witch and the Wardrobe,* which had been published the previous year
- identification of the book as a children's book
- emphasis on the adventure and fantasy dimensions of the book
- praise of Lewis's artistry as a writer
- acknowledgement of the religious orientation of the book
- general agreement that the book was an outstanding literary achievement

Anonymous. "C. S. Lewis's Children's Classic." *The Church Times,* **November 30, 1951.**

- "This year, in *Prince Caspian,* [Lewis] has scored another winner [alongside *LWW*]—but not by quite so long a head."
- "The two books *[PC* and *LWW]* must be seen together if the reader, old or young, is to discover Mr. Lewis's intention. For the books, if they are magical, are at the same time parables. They deal mostly with dwarfs and talking animals. But they are simultaneously about the Christian religion."
- "But let no one suppose that this volume, any more than its predecessor, is just pious precept. *Prince Caspian* is a first-rate story. It is written for children, and it is childlike. The adventures carry suspense. . . . The whole is written in beautiful English. Let any parent start reading the book aloud, and see how an English children's story should be written."

- "Are there criticisms? Unfortunately, in this volume, yes. There is more myth than before, and a lot too much bacchanalia. Nor has Mr. Lewis retained the unities as carefully as he did before. But this is a book which will live. With its earlier companion, it will be a children's classic, and be handed down to children's children."

Anonymous. Untitled review. *Saturday Review*, November 19, 1951, pp. 70-71.
- "This is a sequel to 'The Lion, the Witch and the Wardrobe.' "
- "Boys and girls who enjoyed the first book will find here the same reward: a good plot, convincing characters, and the graceful wording that distinguishes this writer."
- "Adults reading it will be reminded in some phrases of his 'The Screwtape Letters.' "

Anonymous. Untitled review. *Booklist* 48 (December 1951): 131.
- "This sequel has the same spell-binding, magical quality, and good writing but lacks most of the grimness of the other book [LWW] which should be read first for full understanding and enjoyment."
- Grades 4-7.

Anonymous. Untitled review. *The Junior Bookshelf* 15 (December 1951): 276.
- "It is a picturesque, romantic story, with hints here and there of Dr. Lewis's erudition and deeper facts of his talents."
- "The canvas is a little crowded, but the colourful story and fine writing carry the reader over all obstacles."
- "This is a notable book in some ways which will appeal to the imaginative child who allows himself to be borne away on wings of fantasy."

Bechtel, Louise S. "Come Hither! Hear the Magic Horn! A Dragon

Waits." *New York Herald Tribune Book Review,* November 11, 1952, p. 5.

- "It is a wonderfully well written tale for boys who like dwarves, ancient treasures, 'sorcery and wickedness,' and for those girls who, like Lucy, can remember the time when trees could talk."
- "This sequel is better than 'The Lion, the Witch and the Wardrobe,' in being easier reading with a simpler plot."
- "Here we have style and imagination as seldom met in modern books."
- "The unique sort of excitement and beauty of concepts will overcome, for intelligent children, any extra strangeness of symbolism."

Brady, Charles A. "Book Reviews." *Renascence* 4 (spring 1951): 182-84.

- The review makes comparison to *The Lion, the Witch and the Wardrobe,* but *Prince Caspian* is not called a sequel.
- In this second book "the work of redemption goes on."
- "It must be freely confessed that, when measured against its more radiant predecessor, *Prince Caspian* has little to offer that is utterly new."
- Lewis "delves much deeper" than Kenneth Grahame, Rudyard Kipling and Beatrix Potter "into what might properly be styled the metaphysic of the animal creation."
- "There is always a saga echo in the imaginative writing of Lewis; a taste of the ash-spear; a relish of the barrow."
- The "moral" that emerges is "that goodness is always having to go underground and yet that, in the end, it always triumphs over evil."

Fenner, Phyllis. Untitled review. *Library Journal,* December 15, 1951, p. 2123.

- "Plenty of excitement and the children have real personalities, but I can't believe the average child will like it."
- "For older fairy-tale age."

Walsh, Chad. "Fairyland Revisited." *New York Times Book Review,* November 11, 1951, p. 26.

- "This sequel to an earlier adventure in fairyland . . . has the same down-to-earth qualities."
- "The story is for boys and girls who like their dwarfs and fauns as solid as the traffic policeman on the corner."
- "The present book has a more complicated structure than the first one. I suspect that some children will have difficulty following the story-within-a-story that develops."
- Comparison is made between Lewis and MacDonald: "the sense of poetic magic and wonder which Macdonald could evoke is not found in 'Prince Caspian,' but both writers share a deep respect for children and the world of the child's imagination."

℮ 19 ℮

The Critics Comment on
Prince Caspian

The purpose of the following survey of critical commentary on *Prince Caspian* is to provide further helpful avenues by which to explore Lewis's story. The ideas summarized below point readers toward resources that can facilitate additional reflection and discussion beyond what we have already provided in the reader's guide section of this book. We have distilled what is most useful along these lines from the sources we have surveyed. All of these resources are available for use at the Marion E. Wade Center, Wheaton College, and many are obtainable from your local public library via interlibrary loan.

Christopher, Joe R. *C. S. Lewis.* **Boston: Twayne, 1987.**
In a one-page treatment the author condenses useful information about the climactic battle: the individual combat ends in general conflict; the climax of the battle draws upon the Tolkienian and ancient folklore motif of walking trees (also used by Shakespeare in *Macbeth*); the treatment of the woods here and elsewhere in the book represents a classical motif in the book.

Cox, David Randolph. "Elements of Fairy Story in C. S. Lewis's Chronicles of Narnia." Master's thesis, University of Florida, 1978.
The elements of fairy story in *Prince Caspian* include the following: the Telmarines' associating their fears of woods and water with ghosts; Trumpkin's telling the story of Caspian to children around a campfire; talking animals and *Longaevi* (a generic term for medieval fairies of many types); the failure of older siblings on a quest combined with the superior performance of a younger sibling; leaving an object behind (in this case Edmund's flashlight) in the fairy world to hint at a connection between that world and ours (and also indicate a possible future return to the fairy world).

Downing, David C. *Into the Wardrobe: C. S. Lewis and the Narnia Chronicles.* **San Francisco: Jossey-Bass, 2005.**
An exploration of the manipulation of time in Narnia. The *literary* significance of the differential between earthly time and time in Narnia (where events unfold with virtually no corresponding lapse of time on earth) is that it allows us to experience all of Narnia's history within a short span of earthly existence. The *spiritual* significance of this relationship of earthly and Narnian time is that the technique embodies Lewis's faith in a transcendent God who stands outside ordinary time.

Edwards, Bruce L. *Not a Tame Lion.* **Wheaton, Ill.: Tyndale, 2005.**
Mentoring in valor and righteousness is the thematic center of the story. Caspian's greatest trait is humility. He wisely surrounds himself with trust-

worthy counselors who can help him see rightly. The truths that Caspian and others in the story must learn are founded upon ancient knowledge; however, these truths are no less valuable or valid because of their age. There are consequences to lost perspective, and trustworthy friends are essential to the ability to discern truth from falsehood.

Ford, Paul F. "Prince Caspian: The Return to Narnia." In *The C. S. Lewis Readers' Encyclopedia*. Edited by Jeffrey D. Schultz and John G. West Jr. Grand Rapids: Zondervan, 1998, pp. 337-39.

This story introduces some "great Narnian characters," including Trumpkin, Caspian and Reepicheep. Among the book's themes are (1) the question of whether the Christian faith is still true or only something that happened long ago, and (2) the use and misuse of nature and people. One of the links between *Prince Caspian* and some of Lewis's nonfictional writings is his exploration of the psychological problems involved in believing the Christian faith.

Foulon, Jacqueline. "The Theology of C. S. Lewis's Children's Books." Master's thesis, Fuller Theological Seminary, 1962.

The theological themes of the book include the following: the character of Aslan/Christ; the conflict between good and evil; the growth of a soul in knowledge of Jesus.

Gibson, Evan K. *C. S. Lewis: Spinner of Tales*. Washington, D.C.: Christian University Press, 1980.

The discussion covers the topics of characterization, plot and themes. In *Prince Caspian* Lewis created a gallery of memorable characters, all of whom are moral *exempla* (good or bad) who display individualizing personality traits as well. Aslan guides and protects his followers, but creatures must perform on their own the tasks they are given. The plot falls into five sections: (1) discovery of the ruined state of Narnia as it currently exists; (2) the history of Caspian in his youth; (3) the journey to Aslan's How; (4) the battle; and (5) restoration of Narnia. The two main themes are faith in an age of doubt and the rule of the human race over nature.

Glover, Donald E. C. S. Lewis: The Art of Enchantment. Athens: Ohio University Press, 1981.
The narrative structure rests on the contrast between two worlds—Old Narnia and the Narnia that has degenerated to its present state as the kingdom of Miraz. The second of these worlds also encompasses the modern world that we ourselves know. The main theme is belief, as every major character either readily accepts the truth about Aslan and Old Narnia, tests and then accepts it, or rejects it outright. The test of faith in Aslan is the central issue of the book, and Lucy emerges as a hero of belief and obedience. Glover is critical of many of the narrative strategies we implicitly praise in the reader's guide section of this book, such as the ways in which expectations that have been raised are not fulfilled as anticipated (e.g., Narnia is not reclaimed in battle by Caspian but is reclaimed by the power of Aslan) and the alternation between scenes of *agon* (conflicts or struggle) and celebration. He sees humor as a noteworthy ingredient of the book.

Guroian, Vigen. *Tending the Heart of Virtue: How Classic Stories Awaken a Child's Moral Imagination.* New York: Oxford University Press, 1998, pp. 160-70.
Lucy, one of two principal heroes in *Prince Caspian,* is an example of the power of faith. In Christian hagiography St. Lucy is the patron saint of those afflicted in the eyes, and in *Prince Caspian* Lucy is preeminently the one who *sees.* The many references to Lucy's ability to see (and others coming to see what she observes) add up to a picture of religious faith.

Hinten, Marvin D. "Allusions and Parallels in C. S. Lewis's Narnian Chronicles." Ph.D. dissertation, Bowling Green State University, 1997.

Among the allusions that Hinten finds in *Prince Caspian* are the following: the Pevensie siblings' counting steps to locate the treasure chamber at Cair Paravel as an echo of a Sherlock Holmes story; Prince Caspian's nurse and Lewis's own nurse, Lizzie Endicott; the tower on the castle roof to which Dr. Cornelius takes Prince Caspian as reminiscent of the tower of Magdalen College, Oxford, where Lewis taught; Miraz's murdering of Caspian's father to gain the throne as similar to Claudius's murder of Hamlet's father in Shakespeare's play; events late in the story that echo miracles of Jesus in the Gospels.

Johnston, Richard. "The Child Mystic: Transcendence in *Prince Caspian.*" Unpublished paper, Marion E. Wade Center, n.d.
The author identifies Lucy as a child mystic, chiefly on the basis of chapters nine through eleven. These chapters begin "with a beautiful vision as the child mystic," Lucy, wanders at night through a forest. The second vision is Lucy's seeing Aslan and becoming "transfigured." In this second scene Lucy "suddenly moves into the visionary world of the mystic and sees Aslan." The last portion of this unit deals with the aftermath of Lucy's experience. It relates Lucy's experiences to mystical traditions and in more general terms clarifies the spiritual significance of the section of the story that is perhaps the most directly spiritually oriented part of the book.

Karkainen, Paul A. *Narnia Explored.* Old Tappan, N.J.: Revell, 1979.
This work covers divergent topics in a substantial way. The world of the story is in significant ways a medieval world of castles, kings, battles and social customs that prevailed in the Middle Ages. The talking animals, hated by the Telmarines because they belong to Old Narnia, are portrayed by Lewis as having individualizing traits and personalities. The journey of the Pevensie children and Trumpkin is a vehicle for their individual intellectual and spiritual development, and furthermore the journey embodies much of the religious meaning of the story. The Dwarfs Trumpkin and Nikabrik are foils to each other—the skeptic who comes to faith versus the incorrigibly

evil person. Wild nature is a leading value in the story, while civilization is suspect.

Knight, Gareth. *The Magical World of the Inklings*. Longmead, U.K.: Element, 1990.
The main story motif is the royal initiation process, ending with the bestowal of knighthood on Prince Caspian, an act that is also a conferment of spiritual grace. The chivalric trappings are not mere story qualities but are also symbols of the book's deeper themes. The primary underlying theme of the book is belief versus disbelief. A subservient theme is the contrast between relying on one's own judgment and being open to guidance. The incorporation of Bacchus into the Christian vision of the story is part of Lewis's harmonizing of Christianity and paganism. When Caspian takes up the kingship, it is the culmination of a process of faith rather than an act of self-sufficiency. The "divine magic" of Aslan is that he puts "all things right."

Lindskoog, Kathryn. *Journey into Narnia*. Pasadena, Calif.: Hope, 1998.
This is not a unified discussion of the book but rather a collection of individual insights and pieces of information. Examples include the following: feasting as a leading motif in the story; the door in the air at the end of the story as a symbol of the connection between our world and God's higher reality; the importance of teachers and teaching in *Prince Caspian* and their significance in Lewis's life; the literary lineage of the walking trees in the story (Shakespeare's *Macbeth* and Isaiah 55:12, among others).

Manlove, C. N. *C. S. Lewis: His Literary Achievement*. New York: St. Martin's, 1987, pp. 137-46.
This nine-page general discussion takes up so many topics that it is impossible to cover all its points in a brief summary. Multiple parallels with *The Lion, the Witch and the Wardrobe* are noted. Confusion and its eventual clarification are a leading motif in the book. The characters' relation to their environment

is an important dimension of the story, and the exploration of Narnia itself is a large part of the book. The centrality of nature's power is a leading theme, and as part of that emphasis, the forces of good are closely connected with nature, in contrast to the forces of evil (the Telmarines, for example, hate water and forests). In a pattern reminiscent of Shakespeare's comedies and romances, the progress of Caspian's life is from the court to nature and back to a transformed court. Faith in the unseen is a leading motif in the story.

Manlove, Colin. *The Chronicles of Narnia: The Patterning of a Fantastic World.* New York: Twayne, 1993.

Here the author notes parallels between *Prince Caspian* and its predecessor, *The Lion, the Witch and the Wardrobe,* with *Prince Caspian* declared an inferior work that lacks the seriousness of the earlier book. The theme of displacement (the shaking loose from settled assumptions) takes the form of the Pevensie siblings' feeling of dislocation from their familiar world as well as from the Narnia they had known on their first visit. The dominant mood of the book is interrogative, meaning that both the children and we as readers are confronted with many questions and uncertainties as we progress through the book. The most continuous motif is the return of wild nature. The story contains many instances of long-divided characters meeting each other again (the communal theme). At a political level a kind of democracy is restored to Narnia. A strong sense of geography pervades the book.

Medcalf, Stephen. "The Logic of Adventure." *Times Literary Supplement.* February 1990.

Although this is a review of the BBC dramatization of *Prince Caspian* and *The Voyage of the "Dawn Treader,"* the article makes excellent comments about *Prince Caspian* as a book. The book was composed for "children whose tastes are continuous" with those of adults. *Prince Caspian* is a story of battle and adventure, more legendary than mythic. One of the most moving scenes in the Narnia series is the one in which the children wander for some time in the ancient ruin before realizing that it is Cair Paravel, a scene that illustrates the passing of centuries. The character of Reepicheep embodies autobiographical elements, including Lewis's chivalric spirit, childhood fictions about dressed animals and physical clumsiness combined with romantic dreams.

Myers, Doris T. *C. S. Lewis in Context*. Kent, Ohio: Kent State University Press, 1994.
The analysis covers both the literary form and ideational content of the book. It draws parallels between *Prince Caspian* and *The Lion, the Witch and the Wardrobe,* such as the common theme of the attainment of joy through the love of Aslan and the shared plot structure of the Pevensie siblings' journey to the Stone Table. The second book is more spacious than the first— the children are older and the issues more complex. A large part of the didactic purpose of the book is achieved by the moral models that it offers for approval and disapproval. Whether by positive or negative example, the book affirms the virtues of courtesy, justice and obedience to proper authority. The purpose of Myers's book is to show the intellectual substantiality of Lewis's fiction, so further themes that are identified include good education, people's relationship to nature, proper rulership and the traditional meanings of the bacchanal (the romp of Bacchus).

Rogers, Jonathan. *The World According to Narnia: Christian Meaning in C. S. Lewis's Beloved Chronicles*. New York: Warner Faith, 2005.
The chosen focus is to explore the theme of "myth become fact." At the narrative level this myth is the story of Old Narnia, the country of Aslan. As the story unfolds, the faith of various characters in the myth of Old Narnia is proven and validated. Of course this paradigm is an analogy to the Christian faith as reported in the Bible. Characters in the story struggle with issues of faith and doubt in regard to the myths of Old Narnia in the same way that humans struggle with faith and doubt in connection with the claims of the Christian faith. A subsidiary point is that Lewis's handling of classical

mythology in this story illustrates his views on the old myths as "good dreams" that God sent to the human race as shadows of the truth about God.

Schakel, Peter J. *Reading with the Heart: The Way into Narnia*. Grand Rapids: Eerdmans, 1979; *The Way into Narnia: A Reader's Guide*. Grand Rapids: Eerdmans, 2005.

Schakel views *Prince Caspian* as an initiation story that follows Prince Caspian from his childhood in the nursery to his maturity as the new King of Narnia. Within that archetypal pattern, the chosen focus is the theme of belief versus unbelief—in Aslan and in the stories that are told about Old Narnia. Schakel traces this theme in detail, adducing numerous references to characters who believe or who disbelieve in Aslan and the legends of Narnia. This is of course a metaphor for spiritual belief and unbelief. One of the deft touches is Schakel's claim that Lewis reverses the cliché that "seeing is believing" and shows instead that believing is seeing. The final effect of the book is to deemphasize human heroism in deference to the theme of faith, and the distinctiveness of *Prince Caspian* is said to be "not the heroism of human efforts or achievements but of trust . . . and relying on Another."

ℭ 20 ℑ
A Brief Biography of C. S. Lewis

⬥♔⬥

One of the most popular and influential Christian authors of the twentieth century, Clive Staples Lewis was born on November 29, 1898, in Belfast, northern Ireland. His father, Albert, was a lawyer in the Belfast Police Courts, and his mother, Flora, was the daughter of a prominent Church of

Ireland clergyman. Young Clive's early years were spent in a happy and secure home. His only sibling was a brother, Warren, who was three years his senior. The two boys were close friends from an early age and remained so throughout their lives. As children, they shared a variety of interests and spent many happy hours together, riding bicycles, playing on the beach, drawing, writing stories, reading books and sharing many other activities.

As a young child, Clive "rechristened" himself with the nickname of Jacksie (later shortened to Jack), and it was by this designation that he was henceforth known to his family and close friends. When Jack was nine years old, his much-loved mother fell ill and died from cancer. Understandably this was one of the most painful events of his life. Shortly after this he was sent off to boarding school in England with his brother, Warren. This separation from home at such a difficult time contributed to the gulf that was gradually widening between Albert and his sons. Unfortunately this estrangement was compounded by the fact that the boarding school was a poor one, run by an emotionally unstable headmaster. With cause, Jack and Warren were both miserable during their years as students there.

Eventually, after attending several subsequent schools, Jack ended up studying under a private tutor, W. T. Kirkpatrick, in Great Bookham, Surrey. His years with Kirkpatrick not only were idyllic ones but also were academically rewarding as the teenage Jack benefited greatly from the rigorous educational methods of this brilliant teacher. As a result of Kirkpatrick's excellent instruction, in December 1916 Jack earned a scholarship to University College, Oxford.

A short time after Jack entered the university, however, his studies were interrupted when he was called into active service in the trenches of World War I France. After being wounded at the Battle of Arras in 1918, he was sent back to England to convalesce. Following his discharge he returned to Oxford University, where he performed with excellence in his academic studies, receiving three First Class degrees. He was elected to a Fellowship in English Language and Literature at Magdalen College, Oxford, in 1925, where he remained for almost thirty years. In 1954, toward the end of his teaching years, he accepted a professorship at Magdalene College, Cambridge. Lewis's academic career was a distinguished one, resulting in the publication of numerous scholarly texts, including *The Allegory of Love* (1936), *A Preface to Paradise Lost* (1942), *English Literature in the Sixteenth Century, Excluding Drama* (1954) and *An Experiment in Criticism* (1961).

"[C. S. Lewis] aroused warm affection, loyalty, and devotion in his friends, and feelings of almost equal strength among innumerable persons who knew him only through his books. But he also aroused strong antipathy, disapproval, and distaste among some of his colleagues and pupils, and among some readers. It was impossible to be indifferent to him."

HELEN GARDNER, *CLIVE STAPLES LEWIS: 1898–1963*

Though raised in a Christian home, Lewis had become an atheist during his school days in England. The complete story of his return to the Christian faith as an adult convert is recorded in his autobiography, *Surprised by Joy* (1955). In this account he describes his experiences with "joy"—the term he gave to his feelings of inconsolable longing. He came to realize that these experiences of unsatisfied desire were actually divine intimations that pointed to a reality beyond our material world. In addition, his encounters with works by authors such as George MacDonald and G. K. Chesterton, and his discussions with Christian friends such as J. R. R. Tolkien, helped him to overcome his intellectual and emotional barriers to faith. Lewis returned to a belief in Christianity in 1931.

After becoming a Christian, Lewis determined to use his gifts as a writer to communicate his faith. These publications are among his most far-reaching and influential works. Indeed Lewis's singular ability to use imaginative language to depict and clarify theological truths, coupled with his intentional avoidance of sectarian issues and his accomplished skill at rational argument, enabled him to become a powerful voice for the central realities of the Christian faith. The best known of his apologetic volumes is *Mere Christianity*. Among his fiction, his seven Chronicles of Narnia are classics in the field of children's literature and demonstrate the distinctive capacity of fantasy to embody spiritual truths. Through both his religious prose and his fiction, Lewis not only spoke compellingly to unbelievers, but he was also uniquely gifted in nurturing the faith of fellow Christians.

A longtime bachelor, he was married late in life to an American writer, Joy Davidman, and found great happiness in their union. Sadly, their married life together was brief, as Joy died from cancer three years later. Lewis was grief-stricken by his loss, and he survived his wife by only a few years, dying on November 22, 1963. Some forty years after his death, C. S. Lewis continues to be one of the most widely read and influential authors of our time.

KEY DATES IN THE LIFE OF C. S. LEWIS

1898	Born in Belfast, northern Ireland (November 29)
1908	Death of his mother
1914	Goes to study with private tutor, Kirkpatrick
1917	Begins his studies at Oxford University
1917	In the frontlines of WWI France
1919	Returns to his studies at Oxford
1925	Elected a Fellow of Magdalen College, Oxford
1929	Becomes a theist
1929	Death of his father
1931	Returns to a belief in Christianity
1933	Publishes his first book discussing the Christian faith (*The Pilgrim's Regress*)
1942	Publication of *The Screwtape Letters*
1950	Receives his first letter from Joy Davidman Gresham
1950	Publication of *The Lion, the Witch and the Wardrobe*

1951   Publication of *Prince Caspian*

1952   Publication of *Mere Christianity*

1952   Publication of *The Voyage of the "Dawn Treader"*

1953   Publication of *The Silver Chair*

1954   Publication of *The Horse and His Boy*

1955   Takes up Chair of Medieval and Renaissance English at Cambridge University

1955   Publication of *The Magician's Nephew*

1955   Publication of his autobiography, *Surprised by Joy*

1956   Marries Joy Davidman Gresham in a civil ceremony (April 23)

1956   Joy is diagnosed with cancer (October)

1956   Publishes his seventh and final volume of the Chronicles of Narnia (*The Last Battle*)

1957   Marries Joy in an Anglican ceremony at her hospital bedside (March 21)

1960   Death of his wife, Joy Lewis (July 13)

1960   Publication of *The Four Loves*

1961   Publication of *A Grief Observed*

1963   Death of C. S. Lewis (November 22)

Appendix A

The film version of C. S. Lewis's first Narnian story, *The Chronicles of Narnia: The Lion, the Witch and the Wardrobe,* was a great commercial success by any standard. Directed by Andrew Adamson and produced through the joint efforts of Walden Media and Disney, the movie premiered in London on December 9, 2005, and closed May 11, 2006. During its release it grossed $291,710,957 in the United States alone, with an additional $453,073,000 coming from international receipts (easily recouping its reported $180,000,000 production budget). At the end of April 2006 the movie was rated the twentieth highest-grossing film ever in the United States. Not surprisingly, the DVD of the film was also a bestseller upon its release.

The movie version of *The Lion, the Witch and the Wardrobe* was well received for its artistic qualities as well. Critics were generally positive, and the movie was honored with a 2006 Academy Award for Best Achievement in Makeup as well as nominated for its special effects, which were created by WETA Workshop. Rated PG, the film runs two hours and twelve minutes.

Even though the Disney/Walden Media production of *The Lion, the Witch and the Wardrobe* was the first version of C. S. Lewis's classic tale made for release to the big screen, three other creative adaptations for television preceded it. The first of these was a live-action black-and-white presentation that employed people in animal costumes. Produced by ABC Television and shown in Great Britain over ITV, it was broadcast in nine episodes of twenty minutes each, from July through September 1967. Though C. S. Lewis never saw this dramatization (he died in 1963), his brother, Warren, viewed it and recorded the following comments in his diary: "On Television last night I saw the opening installment of Jack's [C. S. Lewis's family nickname] *Lion, Witch and Wardrobe* by which I was agreeably surprised . . . so far it's very promising and I think J would have been pleased with it—no hint so far of what he feared, a touch of Disneyland. . . . The scenery was first rate, and there really was something of magic about the transition from the wardrobe to the dim lit snow covered Narnia."

Following this first effort, an animated version was made by Steve and Bill Melendez as a joint production of the Episcopal Radio-TV Foundation of Atlanta, Georgia, and the Children's Television Workshop of New York. The Emmy Award–winning program consisted of two parts (of one-hour duration each) and was broadcast in April 1979. The first British broadcast of this program occurred in April 1980 on ITV.

A second live-action television series, this time in color, was coproduced by BBC-TV and the American PBS series *Wonderworks* in 1988. Without a major budget for special effects (and long before the technological advances of modern filmmaking), by necessity this program also resorted to the device of using human actors in costumes to portray the inhabitants of Narnia. The first program of *The Lion, the Witch and the Wardrobe* was followed by adaptations of three other Narnian books (*Prince Caspian, The Voyage of the "Dawn Treader"* and *The Silver Chair*).

In this section we have included a cross-section of reviews of the Disney/Walden movie, including those that are favorable and those that are not. It is worth noting that some of the negative reviews reflect the reviewer's dislike of Lewis's original story as much as they are critiques of the film itself:

In his film, Adamson doesn't perceive "Narnia" as just a figment of the
children's imagination, a place they retreat to in their minds to escape
the horrors of World War II. In his conception, Narnia is not like "The
Wizard of Oz" or "Peter Pan," where we realize in the end that the

story happened in someone's imagination. Instead, Adamson creates Narnia as a true alternate universe, using all his resources to show that, when Lucy goes through that wardrobe, the world she enters is completely believable as another country, a Narnian reality unto itself. . . . This film was shot entirely in chronological order, so that with each new scene, the young actors [move] deeper into their characters and further into the discovery of Narnia. This strategy, which is logistically a nightmare and thus seldom used, helped to create a strong family dynamics and unity among the quartet of children. (Emanuel Levy, Emanuellevy.com, December 2005)

One of the most magical effects in Andrew Adamson's *The Lion, the Witch and the Wardrobe* isn't rippling computer-generated fur, ice castles, or battle scenes. It's the wide-eyed wonder and delight on the face of young Lucy Pevensie (Georgie Henley) as she passes beyond the wardrobe for the first time into the winter wonderland of the Narnian wood. . . . The arrival of LWW on the big screen is a cultural milestone of sorts, in some ways a crossroads of *The Lord of the Rings, Harry Potter,* and *The Passion of the Christ.* . . . The film follows the basic plot and structure of the book, and its most important themes—guilt and expiation, sacrifice and redemption, death and resurrection, the triumphs of good over evil—are preserved. Yet widespread reports of the film's "slavish" or "religious" fidelity to the book are just flat wrong. . . . The truth is that the filmmakers have taken significant liberties— some good, some bad, some indifferent. . . . On the whole, though, the filmmakers are safest sticking close to Lewis's story, and tend to go awry when they depart from it. . . . Take the depiction of Peter Pevensie, the eldest sibling, whom Lewis depicts as a natural leader who intuitively grasps the obligation the siblings have to Tumnus and to Narnia. In the film, Peter becomes a reluctant participant who is always trying to back out of Narnian affairs and get his siblings safely back to

England. It's the Aragorn Complex; the only good leader, Hollywood is sure, is a reluctant leader. . . . Other changes are even more ill-advised, and sap Lewis's story of much of its underlying meaning and thematic richness. Most seriously, Aslan, the great and terrible Lion, is robbed of much of his awe-inspiring majesty—not by inherent limitations in translating the story to the screen, but by specific alterations in the screenplay that consistently eliminate references to Aslan's power and his effect on others. . . . The screenplay systematically elevates the role of the children and the Witch herself at Aslan's expense. . . . Visually, Adamson has obviously been influenced by Jackson's trend-setting work in LOTR. As a storyteller, though, Adamson lacks the poetic and dramatic sensibilities that made Jackson's films so effective. The visual and emotional impact of some of the most important sequences, which a more gifted or experienced storyteller would have played for maximum impact, has been muted or lost. . . . Take the transition from the Witch's winter to Aslan's spring, a major motif in the book. . . . Lewis devotes pages and pages to melting snow, running water, the appearance of various varieties of flowers, and so on. The film, however, has no time for all this, and gets it out of the way with an action scene, a few brief effects shots, and a quick transition. . . . All these missteps add up to the difference between what could easily have been one of the greatest family films of all time, and what is, instead, merely a good one. Though the film misses greatness, even in this diminished form Lewis's story is still well worth seeing, and the film adds enough to the experience to keep things fresh. (Stephen D. Greydanus, *Decent Films Guide,* December 2005)

"The Chronicles of Narnia: The Lion, the Witch and the Wardrobe" displays an abiding respect for its source, C. S. Lewis's beloved fantasy classic. . . . What's missing is an excitement that I looked for and didn't find. Nor did I find the religious content intrusive—why shouldn't a fantasy have deeper resonance?—but I wonder if respect for Lewis's legacy led the filmmakers to undue earnestness. That's not to say that this first visit to a live-action Narnia on screen isn't enjoyable. . . . But there's not a lot of humor along the way, and the epic struggle between good and evil plays out in battles more impressive than thrilling. On the other hand, how can your heart not melt when, at the end of the Sturm und Drang, Aslan, risen again, begins a coronation ceremony with the ringing words: "I give you Queen Lucy the Valiant." (Joe Morgenstern, *Wall Street Journal,* December 9, 2005)

While much has been made of this story's Christian roots, Adamson's restrained approach ensures that they are, like Narnia, only evident to the faithful. What most viewers will see instead is a straightforward exploration of good and evil, friendship and family, and courage and cowardice. . . . What great epic doesn't rely on these grand themes? . . . The movie is not entirely seamless: Some of the computer-animated animals are too cute, and we do catch that digitalized backdrop more than once. But there's hardly time to notice flaws, since Adamson keeps us thoroughly entranced with spectacles like the teeming Narnian battlefield, on which a jaw-dropping army of minotaurs, centaurs and unicorns gathers. . . . Most magical of all is the beautifully natural interaction among the children, each of whom breathes palpable life into Lewis's gently empathetic text. (Elizabeth Weitzman, *New York Daily News,* December 8, 2005)

In a recently discovered note by C. S. Lewis, from 1959, he wrote: "Anthropomorphic animals, when taken out of narrative into actual visibility, always turn into buffoonery and nightmare." . . . Which is exactly what doesn't happen in "The Chronicles of Narnia: the Lion, The Witch and The Wardrobe"—at least not the buffoonery part. . . . Andrew Adamson, the director of the two "Shrek" films, has done a highly creditable job of visualizing the first of 'Lewis's seven books about four children in the mythical land of Narnia where the animals do, indeed, talk. . . . The film, which is much closer in look to the book's illustrations by Pauline Baynes than might have been predicted, works surprisingly well both as a boisterous fantasia and as the Christian fable that Lewis intended. (Peter Rainer, *Christian Science Monitor,* December 9, 2005)

It's taken more than 50 years for a live-action version of Christian author C. S. Lewis' beloved children's fantasy, "The Lion, the Witch and the Wardrobe," to finally make it to the big screen. And after viewing Disney's captivating $150 million adaptation, it's safe to say it was well worth the wait. . . . Produced in partnership with faith-friendly Walden Media, the movie not only stays reverently true to the story and spiritual subtext of Lewis' imaginative tale, but is a cinematic work of extraordinary beauty that, much like the title's enchanted armoire, transports viewers to a wondrous world of adventure, heroism and religious symbolism. . . . It also proves what Lewis believed about literature—that anything worth reading when you are 5 is worth reading when you are 50—is equally valid for film, though Lewis himself had strong reservations about translating his Narnia books into live-action movies. (*United States Conference of Catholic Bishops,* January 25, 2006)

As many readers already know, there are two ways to approach *The Chronicles of Narnia: The Lion, the Witch and the Wardrobe.* . . . The first is as a plain-faced fantasy. . . . The second involves seeing it as the Christian allegory it truly is. . . . Is it of interest, however, to separate the two approaches in a discussion of the movie? I might say only in one respect—the books and, thus, the movie are aimed at children, and children are not likely to draw Christian parallels from a film that features colorful visual effects, a wide range of characters, and new lands to explore. Therefore, one has some room to talk about it as a pure work of fantasy, and yet this is where *Narnia* falters. As a story, it's surprisingly shallow because it's so intent on sticking to its agenda that character believability—possibly more important in fantasies than in other genres since it provides the only real grounding—suffers as a result. . . . To watch *Narnia* is to observe a promise of rich fantasy ultimately hampered by its insistence on delivering a very specific, pre-defined story simply dressed up in ornate clothing. It begins with a brood of four children. . . . Their personalities are lightly drawn, and they eventually happen upon a portal to a magical world. The potential for story here is most ripe. However, once the tale begins to develop, the main characters take a backseat to arbitrary events. They become ciphers the minute someone explains that they are prophesied to rule the land—they no longer make stuff happen, stuff just happens to them. (Jeffrey Chen, *ReelTalk Movie Reviews,* December 12, 2005)

This isn't a Christian movie, and in fact if Disney wasn't going out of their way to market the thing directly to church groups hoping for a *Passion of the Christ* cash-in, you wouldn't notice any sort of Christ connection while watching it. . . . What *The Chronicles of Narnia: The Lion, the Witch and the Wardrobe* really is, is a spectacular adaptation of a fairly nice fantasy tale. It doesn't just live up to its source material, it surpasses it by finding nuances in the story that C. S. Lewis didn't. That's not to say there's been anything added. Director Andrew Adamson follows a path that for the most part, sticks almost slavishly to the details of the book. But in between those details he finds emotional depth and resonance that isn't obviously there in the short, rather simplistic children's novel written by Lewis. . . . The only serious flaw with the film is the effects, which look at times half done or rushed. I'm not saying the computer generated creatures don't look good, they do. This is a beautiful movie. The designs are interesting and believable, if nowhere near photorealistic. However, a lot of the time *Narnia's* great computer generated creatures don't blend in properly with the live action shots. . . . The CGI characters often look like they've been overlaid on the film, rather than appearing as something that we can accept as living in it. It's more an issue of how these CGI creations (of which there are many in the film) interact with their environment. The thing is, for the most part, they don't. . . . Minute effects issues aside, this is otherwise a fantastic, affecting film with real thought and love for the material behind it. It's full of wide-eyed wonder and innocent delight, a different kind of fantasy from that found in the other great material we've seen from the genre as of late. C. S. Lewis's thinly developed novel leaves plenty of room for Adamson to let his imagination wild. With his help, *Narnia* takes flight. (Joshua Tyler, *Cinema Blend,* December 9, 2005)

In the weeks leading up to the release of "The Chronicles of Narnia: The Lion, the Witch and the Wardrobe," the entertainment press has sometimes seemed so preoccupied with matters of allegory as to resemble an advanced seminar in Renaissance literature. . . . It has never been a secret that C. S. Lewis, who taught that subject and others at Oxford for many years, composed his great cycle of seven children's fantasy novels with the New Testament in mind and with some of the literary traditions it inspired close at hand. To the millions since the 1950's for whom the books have been a source of childhood enchantment, Lewis's religious intentions have either been obvious, invisible or beside the point. . . . Anyone who grew up with the Narnia books is likely to be concerned less with Lewis's beliefs than with the filmmakers' fidelity to his work, which was idiosyncratic and imperfect in ways that may not easily lend themselves to appropriation by the shiny and hyperkinetic machinery of mass visual fantasy. But if a few liberties have been taken here and there, as is inevitable in the transition from page to screen, the spirit of the book is very much intact. . . .

"The Lion, the Witch and the Wardrobe" suggests that, at least in Hollywood, there is no such thing as too much Englishness. . . . For me, the best moments in the film take place in the wardrobe itself, which serves as a portal between England and Narnia. When the children pass through it for the first time, I felt a welcome tremor of apprehension and anticipation as the wooden floor turned into snowy ground and fur coats gave way to fir trees. The next two hours might not have quite delivered on that initial promise of wonder—we grown-ups, being heavy, are not so easily swept away by visual tricks—except when I looked away from the screen at the faces of breathless and wide-eyed children, my own among them, for whom the whole experience was new, strange, disturbing and delightful. (A. O. Scott, *New York Times,* December 9, 2005)

The Chronicles of Narnia: The Lion, the Witch and the Wardrobe is more than just a mouthful, it's a franchise killer. Disney has spared no expense in bringing the first installment of C. S. Lewis' beloved seven-book series to the screen, but they've given us no reason to want to visit Narnia ever again . . . the movie is a leaden, slow-moving beast. Director Andrew Adamson, who co-helmed the *Shrek* series before getting in over his head with live action, clearly takes enormous pleasure in designing centaurs and Cyclopes, werewolves and fauns, but he captures none of the narrative charm or personality of Lewis' source material. Gone is the benevolent old storyteller eager to stimulate our imagination, replaced by a personality-devoid treatment that locks Lewis' vision to the stage of CG circa 2005. (Peter Debruge, *Premiere Magazine,* December 9, 2005)

There are several things to be grateful for in Disney's adaptation of "The Chronicles of Narnia: The Lion, the Witch and the Wardrobe," which, considering how beloved the source, comes as a relief. Most people who read the C. S. Lewis series as kids recall it with a fierce and proprietary fondness. But aside from an added prologue that kicks off the story in London and helps to ground it in a reality against which to contrast the fantasy to come, the movie remains faithful to the book in both tone and imagery. . . . If it weren't for Lewis' stated intention to write a fantastical story to make the dogma go down, it might even come across as liberal humanist parable about myth and its function in society, especially during times of trouble. (Carina Chocano, *Los Angeles Times*, December 7, 2005)

The kids are from a tradition which requires that British children be polite and well-spoken, no doubt because Lewis preferred them that way. What is remarkable is that this bookish bachelor who did not marry until he was nearly 60 would create four children so filled with life and pluck. . . . That's the charm of the Narnia stories: They contain magic and myth, but their mysteries are resolved not by the kinds of rabbits that Tolkien pulls out of his hat, but by the determination and resolve of the Pevensie kids—who have a good deal of help, to be sure, from Aslan the Lion. . . . The adventures that Lucy has in Narnia, at first by herself, then with her brother Edmund and finally with the older Peter and Susan, are the sorts of things that might happen in any British forest, always assuming fauns, lions and witches can be found there, as I am sure they can. Only toward the end of this film do the special effects ramp up into spectacular extravaganzas that might have caused Lewis to snap his pipe stem. . . . These events, fantastical as they sound, take place on a more human, or at least more earthly, scale than those in "Lord of the Rings." . . . C. S. Lewis famously said he never wanted the Narnia books to be filmed because he feared the animals would "turn into buffoonery or nightmare." But he said that in 1959, when he might have been thinking of a man wearing a lion suit, or puppets. . . . The effects in this movie are so skillful that the animals look about as real as any of the other characters, and the critic Eman-

uel Levy explains the secret: "Aslan speaks in a natural, organic manner (which meant mapping the movement of his speech unto the
whole musculature of the animal, not just his mouth)." . . . It's remarkable isn't it, that the Brits have produced Narnia, the Ring, Hogwarts,
Gormenghast, James Bond, Alice and Pooh, and what have we produced for them in return? (Roger Ebert, *Rogerebert.com,* movie review,
December 8, 2005)

You can read the seven volumes of *The Chronicles of Narnia* as a Christian allegory or as an ornate book of wonder (or both), but either way
it's marked by the devout, almost pristine earnestness of Lewis' sincer-
ity and gravitas. Narnia, a land of fauns, talking beavers, a dastardly
White Witch, and a solemn savior of a lion, may sound like the stuff of
filigreed fairy tales, but it's really a place of holy war, where the imagination darkens the more it expands. . . . In the lavish, spirited, at times
naggingly literal-minded movie version of the hugely popular first *Narnia* tale, you're often aware that you're watching child actors romp
through a land of concocted creatures and special effects. . . . Yet the
movie, for all its half-baked visual marvels, remains remarkably faithful
to Lewis' story, and the innocence of his passion begins to shine
through. It's there, most spectacularly, in Aslan, the lion-king messiah.
For once, a computerized beast looks like he's talking, and he's voiced,
by Liam Neeson, in velvet seductive tones of lordly compassion.
(Owen Gleiberman, *Entertainment Weekly,* December 7, 2005)

Richer, stranger "Narnia" pictures than this disappointing inaugural
effort may well be forthcoming. . . . But too often in "The Lion, the
Witch and the Wardrobe," even with a good cast and a promising first
hour, the results recall the subtitle of "The Pirates of Penzance," the
old Gilbert and Sullivan operetta: "The Slave of Duty." This project is
a slave of duty. It tells Lewis' story, which has its share of sticky and
ponderous aspects, in a predictable, visually cautious way. You keep

waiting to be transported, yet in cinematic terms, the transportation never arrives. . . . The premise itself remains a thing of simple, graceful power; even if you're not into the overt Christian aspects of Lewis' allegory. . . . The early forays into Narnia are handled with a fetchingly modest sense of wonder. For a long time the movie does not feel like a zillion-dollar attempt at a blockbuster. . . . The problem with "The Lion, the Witch and the Wardrobe" is this: The closer the many-hands screenplay gets to the Christ-like sufferings and the resurrection of Lord Aslan, the lion (voiced by Liam Neeson), the more conflicted the filmmakers' efforts become. In Lewis' book, 85 pages long, the climactic battle of good versus evil—Aslan and his followers on one side, the White Witch and her unholy supporters on the other—is dispatched in a few sentences. Here it's a full-on, major-league blow-out, though more numbing than vivid. . . . The film itself doesn't feel ripe so much as fresh-frozen, designed to preserve all the narrative events of the original without bothering enough about the flavor. (Michael Phillips, *Chicago Tribune,* December 8, 2005)

Like the "The Lord of the Rings," C. S. Lewis' "The Chronicles of Narnia: The Lion, the Witch and the Wardrobe" was the product of a Great Britain that had just been through a war of survival. The story neither was about World War II, nor was it an allegory for it, and yet it was informed by the moral absolutes and challenges of the wartime period: There's the presence of darkest evil, which can't be avoided but must be faced head-on. There's the grim understanding that sacrifice is necessary, that whole worlds are riding on the actions of a handful of individuals. And, in the presence of a wickedness so complete as to be supernatural, there's faith in absolute goodness. . . . Except for "The Lord of the Rings" trilogy, there's no philosophical precedent for this kind of film in recent cinema: The idea that life might even have an ultimate meaning goes against the modern trend. . . . That the film is a Christian allegory is beyond dispute. This element is in no way disguised, nor should it be, as it's a major source of the story's power. It functions in two distinct ways. The allegory elevates the tale to the monumental scale of salvation and damnation. And it shows the eternal application of the Christian metaphor, working in the Miltonian sense to "justify the ways of God to man." Thus, despite its enormous secular appeal, "The Chronicles of Narnia" could also be called the most effective and moving religious picture since Nick Ray's "King of Kings." (Mick Lasalle, *San Francisco Chronicle,* December 9, 2005)

For decades, CS Lewis' book series The Chronicles of Narnia has had children bumping their heads into the backs of old cupboards looking for a winter wonderland populated by fauns, centaurs and talking beavers. A movie version of *The Lion, The Witch And The Wardrobe* feels long overdue and, while it's not seamless, that seductive aura of magic, mystery and menace remains intact. As the cold-hearted White Witch, Tilda Swinton sets the tempo for this bracing adventure. She is a pristine picture of evil like the spectre of Nazism that forces the Pevensie children out of London and to the sanctuary of a country manor. . . . Providing the laughs are Ray Winstone and Dawn French as a pair of bickering beavers, but there's also a sobering edge in visions of death and sacrifice. Adamson handles the balance well for a lesson in courage that melts away all cynicism. (Stella Papamichael, BBC, December 9, 2005)

With an almighty roar, Aslan the lion springs from the clifftop and into the biggest, most breathtaking battle you've ever seen. With griffins screaming overhead, the massive cat swipes aside minotaurs and tigers with a huge paw before squaring up to the evil White Witch, who stands before him astride a silver chariot. Boasting astonishing special effects, great performances from the cast and the wickedest witch of all time, films don't get much better than this. . . . While the epic clash is the highlight of the movie, Narnia is a film brimming with great moments. Shot in New Zealand, all of the book's best bits have been crammed in. And, amid the menace, there's plenty of wry humour. In one scene, Edmund climbs onto a steed and shouts, "Go horsey!" to which the animal calmly replies, "Actually, my name is Phillip." . . . There isn't a bad performance here, with Tilda Swinton's witch making Lord Voldemort from the latest Harry Potter movie look like the school sissy. But the standout is 14-year-old Skandar Keynes as Edmund, who manages the difficult trick of going from bratty brother to reformed hero. . . . The result is movie magic. (David Edwards, *Daily Mirror,* December 2, 2005)

Ever since Hollywood first showed an interest in the Narnia books, fans have feared for their safety. There have been rumours of "Americanisation" and "modernization." It was said there was a script circulating that set Narnia in contemporary America: in this version, one of the children sells his soul to the White Witch not for Turkish delight, but for cheeseburgers. . . . Narnia fans, fear not. This is not one of those Hollywood films that raise your hope, then mug your memories. Disney and the director Andrew Adamson (Shrek) have been faithful to the book and produced something wonderful. In fact, this is perhaps the most English film never to have been made in England. True, most of the action is set in the wintry wonderland of Narnia, a place full of strange beasts: fauns, centaurs, and talking animals. But the film is equally fascinated by another exotic land: England in the 1940s. Here is a strange, mythical place of old country houses, eccentric professors, stiff upper lips and jolly children with bad teeth. . . . Adamson to his credit, has made an epic fantasy for young children. . . . Devoted fans of the book should just shut up, sit back and give this film a chance to work its magic. They won't be disappointed. (Cosmo Landesman, *Sunday Times,* December 4, 2005)

"Lion" functions best as a "Wizard of Oz"-like trip, an expression of innocent, parent-deprived children's imaginative escape from dreary reality into an exquisite but perilous world of starkly personified good and evil dominated by animals, human-like characters and a witch. Like "Oz," it similarly ends with the leads' confounding decision to return to that dull reality rather than to stay in a wondrous land where they are regarded as heroes and royalty. . . . Pic's credibility hinges as much on the visualization of the lion as on anything else. Compared with the wolves, the imposing Aslan looks somewhat less lifelike at first; his expressions seem a bit posed and the waviness of his mane and other hair isn't entirely naturalistic. But one soon accepts him, as his movements carry a deliberate composure and Neeson's sonorous readings convey a steady dignity. . . . Although there are a few obvious process shots and telltale painted backdrops, the film's design elements and special and visual effects are mostly impressive; seemingly the only thing the tech maestros couldn't pull off is making the characters' breath visible in the mostly winter settings. (Todd McCarthy, *Variety.com*, December 4, 2005)

When did Father Christmas become an arms dealer, doling out swords, shields, bows and arrows to the kiddies so they can kill their enemies? . . . Santa's military side-job is one of a few niggling problems besetting "The Chronicles of Narnia: The Lion, the Witch and the Wardrobe," a surprisingly violent, special-effects-packed fantasy that presumably earned a PG rating because hardly anyone bleeds. . . . Much has been made of the Christianity metaphors that Lewis imbedded in his tale. . . . Fortunately, the religious underpinnings of "Chronicles" don't get in the way of its story, still an entertaining yarn despite the wavering CGI quality that vacillates from perfect realism to the subtly artificial animal effects of "Jumanji." (Dan Gire, *Chicago Daily Herald*, December 8, 2005)

It is never too late to honour one's parents, but always too late to honour them enough. That they never read C. S. Lewis's *The Chronicles of Narnia* to me in my childhood showed a wisdom, I now realize, beyond their honest, war-scarred years. I can scarcely remember a more cringe-making two hours in the cinema than this faithful (I am told by Lewisites) rendering of the Christian academic's folklore epic about faith, love and moral rearmament. . . . The film oscillates between the insipid and the sanctimonious. . . . I credit Lewis's original book, or books, with storytelling skill. Something must explain their popularity. But the awfulness of this Disney version . . . is its one-step, two-step pacing and its glutinous pictorialism in the aid of preachiness. (Nigel Andrews, *Financial Times,* December 8, 2005)

CS Lewis's classic of children's fantasy literature, to which six installments of steeply declining interest and power were added, has now been brought to the screen by Andrew Adamson, of Shrek fame. The result is a triumph. It is gorgeous to look at, superbly cast, wittily directed and funny and exciting by turns. It unfolds the slim book into a rich visual experience that is bold and spectacular and sweeping, while retaining its human intimacies. I can't see how it could be done better. . . . There will be many adults like me, who after loving the book as children went through a long post-adolescent phase of hysterically repudiating it after the Christian-humanist parable was explained. For me, it is a phase that this movie has definitively brought to an end. Adamson brings out the story's romantic gallantry and its wonderfully generous approach to childhood. For all the rhapsodic seriousness, and Blakean associations of England with Christianity, the film has a lightness of touch. . . . There is no need for anyone to get into a PC huff about its Christian allegory. With this movie's buoyant fun, Adamson provides something akin to the sense of humor Graham Greene said he needed in order to believe. Although you don't need to believe in a fairytale to find it enchanting. (Peter Bradshaw, *Guardian Unlimited*, December 2, 2005)

There were about a couple of hundred children in the suburban theater to see the "The Lion, the Witch and the Wardrobe," the movie based on one book in the wonderful "Chronicles of Narnia" series by C. S. Lewis. . . . I took my 10-year-old twin boys to see it. The deal was we'd see the film only after they had read the book. They read it, we talked about it, and then the other night, we drove to the theater. . . . And what I saw there amazed me. . . . There wasn't a peep out of all those kids during the movie. . . . There wasn't a sound. Perhaps that's because wonder doesn't have a sound. But I could see it in the eyes of my boys, and in the eyes of the other children. . . . Throughout the movie, I kept peeking at the faces of my sons. They're boys and were attracted to the battles and the action, because boys love movie battles of all kinds, but it wasn't the swordplay and centaurs' cavalry charge that will stick with them. . . . What will stick is the sense of gentle wonder in the film, from the first step through the wardrobe into the snowy land of Narnia, to the first tea and toast served by the faun, to the gracious manner in which most characters addressed each other. (John Kass, *Chicago Tribune*, December 23, 2005)

Appendix B

Using This Guide with Reading Groups

The discussion and reflection questions scattered throughout this reader's guide serve as an excellent starting place for all types of reading groups. Whatever format your group already employs, this volume offers an abundance of resources to enhance your reading of *Prince Caspian* (or any of the other six Narnian books). But, in particular, using the discussion prompts (in the gray-shaded boxes) can help you get the conversation flowing as well as provide members of your group with a variety of topics from which to choose when there are gaps in the discussion. By making use of these reflection questions and the other resources in this guide, members of your group will be led deeper into the story of *Prince Caspian* itself.

In addition, as you use this reader's guide:

- Don't feel that you need to "answer" every question. Skip over those that don't interest you and spend more time on those that do.
- Make use of the background materials offered in this guide, such as the biographical sketch of C. S. Lewis, the boxed sidebars and the excerpts from contemporary reviews and critical commentary. All of these items offer helpful material that will enable you to put *Prince Caspian* in historical and literary context.
- Skim the index of this book to look for topics that are of particular interest to individuals in your group or the group as a whole. This can point you toward aspects of the book you might not have discovered on your own.
- Relax and let the discussion go wherever your group finds beneficial. En-

joyment is the key to truly receiving what story is all about—and the discussion of story should be no less enjoyable.

- Finally, do not spend your time trying to exhaust the specifics of the book, but rather allow the story to stimulate new understanding and insights. Or to put it another way, enter the story imaginatively—as a young child would do—and see where your literary journey will take you. As C. S. Lewis himself advised: with any work of art (literary or otherwise), it is crucial that first of all, we look, listen, surrender and receive, for then "we shall be deliciously surprised by the satisfaction of wants we were not aware of till they were satisfied."

Appendix C

USING THIS GUIDE WITH
HOME SCHOOL STUDENTS

This reader's guide has been intentionally crafted to serve as a self-directed tour of *Prince Caspian*. As a result it is ideally suited to aid a home school student who is accustomed to working independently.

Scattered throughout this book are various sections headed "For Reflection or Discussion." In each of these gray-shaded boxes the reader will find an assortment of suggestions that are offered as a means of leading the student deeper into the story itself. They are further designed to serve as the types of questions that a teacher in a classroom setting would use to facilitate conversation among his or her students.

Please note that we do not recommend that a home school student attempt to "answer" every reflection point in this volume. Rather, just as with any other reader using this guide, it is wise to select those reflection questions that point to areas or topics that the student would particularly benefit from exploring in more depth. Our intention in providing these prompts is to enrich the reading experience, not set a series of examination questions.

In addition the critical commentary (pp. 29-85), the contemporary reviews (pp. 120-24), the survey of critics (pp. 124-32) and the recommended reading list (p. 162) will be of particular assistance to a home school student. These resources offer fruitful avenues for the reader to explore as a means of better understanding *Prince Caspian* as well as the Narnian chronicles as a whole.

Appendix D

Pauline Baynes's Illustrations of *Prince Caspian:*
U.K. First Edition Compared to U.S. First Edition

	Illustration	1st edition British Location	1st edition American Location
1	Lucy frolicking with Narnians	dust jacket front (tinted blue)	dust jacket front (tinted pink)
2	Reepicheep with grapes speared on his sword	dust jacket spine	dust jacket back
3	Silhouette of Caspian and Narnians (adapted from illustration below: "Caspian dances with the Old Narnians")	not used	front hard cover
4	Map of Narnia and adjoining lands	front cover endpapers	*not included*
5	Narnians and Lucy frolicking in woods with Aslan in distance	full color frontispiece	*not included*
6	The Pevensie children surveying the coast	Chapter 1	Chapter 1
7	The Pevensie children rediscover Cair Paravel	Chapter 1	full page (as a frontispiece to Chapter 2)
8	Susan finds the gold chess piece	Chapter 2	Chapter 2
9	The Pevensie children enter the doorway of the castle treasure chamber	Chapter 2	title page
10	Peter and Lucy find their gifts from Father Christmas	Chapter 2	Chapter 2
11	Soldiers in a rowboat with a bundle	Chapter 3	Chapter 3
12	The Dwarf rubs his ankles when freed from the ropes	Chapter 3	*not included*
13	The Pevensies and the Dwarf go fishing in the rowboat	Chapter 3	Chapter 3
14	The stories of Caspian's nurse: Naiads and dryads and talking cats and dogs	Chapter 4	*not included*
15	Dr. Cornelius	Chapter 4	Chapter 4
16	Dr. Cornelius tells Caspian of Old Narnia at night at the top of the Great Tower	Chapter 4	Chapter 4
17	Caspian flees through the woods on his horse Destrier	Chapter 5	*not included*
18	Trufflehunter gives Caspian a cup of something sweet and hot while the Dwarves look on from the fire	Chapter 5	*not included*
19	Three Bulgy Brown Bears wake in the spring	Chapter 5	Chapter 6

	Illustration	1st edition British Location	1st edition American Location
20	Pattertwig, "the most magnificent red squirrel that Caspian had ever seen"	Chapter 6	*not included*
21	Reepicheep makes a dashing and graceful bow	Chapter 6	Chapter 6
22	Caspian dances with the Old Narnians	Chapter 6	Chapter 6
23	Caspian addresses the council of Old Narnians	Chapter 7	*not included*
24	King Miraz's army encamps against the Old Narnians	Chapter 7	Chapter 7
25	Giant Wimbleweather sheds big tears on the mice	Chapter 7	Chapter 7
26	Edward disarms Trumpkin in a fencing match	Chapter 8	Chapter 8
27	The apple pierced by Susan's arrow falls from the bough	Chapter 8	*not included*
28	Lucy looks up to see the nightingale sing	Chapter 9	*not included*
29	Lucy listens for the voices of the trees in the forest	Chapter 9	Chapter 9
30	Lucy tells the other children and the Dwarf of Aslan's guidance up the gorge	Chapter 9	*not included*
31	A hawk flying in the gorge	Chapter 10	*not included*
32	Ferns and a dragonfly at the edge of the river in the gorge	Chapter 10	*not included*
33	The children and Trumpkin crawl along the ground to flee the arrows of Miraz's sentries	Chapter 10	Chapter 10
34	Lucy meets Aslan in the forest	Chapter 10	Chapter 10
35	Aslan shakes Trumpkin in his mouth	Chapter 11	Chapter 11
36	Two rabbits, townsmen, water nymphs, an owl and a hedgehog respond to Aslan's great roar	Chapter 11	*not included*
37	Silenus rides on the donkey while Bacchus and the wild girls caper about with grape vines	Chapter 11	*not included*
38	Trumpkin, Peter and Edmund explore the Mound by torchlight	Chapter 12	Chapter 12
39	Peter, Edmund and Trumpkin find King Caspian, Dr. Cornelius and Trufflehunter fighting off a Wer-Wolf, a Hag and Nikabrik in the Mound	Chapter 12	Chapter 12
40	Lords Glozelle and Sopespian discuss the approach of Edmund with the challenge	Chapter 13	*not included*
41	Trumpkin chastises the Bear for sucking its paws	Chapter 13	Chapter 13
42	Reepicheep threatens anyone who laughs at him with a duel	Chapter 13	Chapter 13
43	The Narnians and the Telmarines look on as Peter and King Miraz fight a duel	Chapter 14	Chapter 14
44	The river-god asks Aslan and the revellers for release	Chapter 14	Chapter 14
45	The revellers and the released animals see a man beating a boy turn into a tree	Chapter 14	*not included*
46	The mice crowd around Reepicheep in readiness to sacrifice their tails like his	Chapter 15	*not included*

	Illustration	1st edition British Location	1st edition American Location
47	A cornucopia of harvested bounty for the feast of celebration	Chapter 15	*not included*
48	The moles bear a feast of dirt to the trees	Chapter 15	Chapter 15
49	A bird perched on a branch calls out the news of Caspian's kingship, while another flies with the message in his beak	Chapter 15	*not included*
50	A Telmarine steps through the door in the air	Chapter 15	Chapter 15
51	The Pevensie children find themselves back on the platform of the country railway station	Chapter 15	Chapter 15

NOTES:

The U.S. edition has 186 pages and the U.K. edition has 195 pages.

The U.S. first edition omits 20 of the 50 illustrations used in the U.K. first edition (those shaded in chart above).

The U.S. version often has slightly smaller versions of the illustrations.

The illustrations in the U.K. edition are more finely printed than those in the U.S. edition.

The U.S. first edition adds one image (adapted from an illustration used later in the book) to the front hard cover that is not used in the U.K. first edition.

Recommended Reading List

In addition to the books surveyed in chapter nineteen, "The Critics Comment on *Prince Caspian*," following are some additional resources to aid you in better understanding C. S. Lewis and *Prince Caspian*.

Duriez, Colin. *A Field Guide to Narnia*. Downers Grove, Ill.: InterVarsity Press, 2004.

Ford, Paul F. *Companion to Narnia*. Rev. ed. San Francisco: HarperSanFrancisco, 2005.

Hein, Rolland. *Christian Mythmakers*. 2nd ed. Chicago: Cornerstone Press Chicago, 2002.

Hooper, Walter. *C. S. Lewis: Companion and Guide*. San Francisco: HarperCollins, 1996.

———. *Past Watchful Dragons*. New York: Collins, 1980.

Kilby, Clyde S. *The Christian World of C. S. Lewis*. Grand Rapids: Eerdmans, 1964.

Lewis, C. S. *Collected Letters*. Edited by Walter Hooper. 3 vols. London: HarperCollins Publishers, 2000-2006.

———. *Letters of C. S. Lewis*. Rev. ed. Edited by Walter Hooper. London: Collins/Fount Paperbacks, 1988.

———. *Letters to Children*. Edited by Lyle W. Dorsett and Marjorie Lamp Mead. New York: Macmillan, 1985.

Ryken, Leland, and Marjorie Lamp Mead. *A Reader's Guide Through the Wardrobe*. Downers Grove, Ill.: InterVarsity Press, 2005.

Schultz, Jeffrey D., and John G. West Jr. *The C. S. Lewis Reader's Encyclopedia*. Grand Rapids: Zondervan, 1998.

Biographical

Dorsett, Lyle W. *A Love Observed: Joy Davidman's Life and Marriage to C. S. Lewis*. Wheaton, Ill.: Harold Shaw, 1998.

Green, Roger Lancelyn, and Walter Hooper. *C. S. Lewis: A Biography*. Rev. ed. London: HarperCollins, 2002.

Jacobs, Alan. *The Narnian: The Life and Imagination of C. S. Lewis*. San Francisco: HarperSanFrancisco, 2005.

Sayer, George. *Jack: A Life of C. S. Lewis*. Wheaton, Ill.: Crossway, 1994.

Notes

Preface

Page 9   "DON'T READ THIS!": J. R. R. Tolkien, "Tolkien's Draft Introduction to *The Golden Key*," in *Smith of Wooton Major,* ed. Verlyn Flieger, extended ed. (London: HarperCollins, 2005), pp. 71-72.

Introduction

Page 14   "The original of this manuscript" (box): Bodleian, Dep. D. 811.

Page 14   "SEQUEL TO L.W.W.": Quoted in Walter Hooper, *C. S. Lewis: A Companion and Guide* (San Francisco: HarperSanFrancisco, 1996), p. 403.

Page 14   "A good idea for a (children's) story": C. S. Lewis, letter to Vera Mathews, September 17, 1949, in *Collected Letters,* ed. Walter Hooper (London: HarperCollins, 2004-2006), 2:980.

Page 18   "The title [finally] adopted": George Sayer, *Jack: A Life of C. S. Lewis* (Wheaton, Ill.: Crossway, 1994), p. 315.

Page 18   "whole series became Christian": Lewis, letter to Sophia Storr, December 24, 1959, in *Collected Letters,* 3:1113.

Page 19   "the old stories about Him": Ibid.

Page 19   "the whole Narnian story is about Christ": Lewis, letter to Anne Waller Jenkins, March 5, 1961, in ibid., 3:1244.

Page 19   "In addition to this general explanation": Ibid., 3:1245.

Page 19   "C. S. Lewis's comment": C. S. Lewis, letter to Lucy, September 11, 1958, in *Letters to Children,* ed. Lyle W. Dorsett and Marjorie Lamp Mead (New York: Macmillan, 1985), p. 81.

Page 19   "It is also interesting to note": Lewis, letter to Kathleen Raine, November 7, 1963, in *Collected Letters,* 3:1478.

Page 24   "The typescript of *Prince Caspian*" ("Children as Narnian Critics" box): Roger Lancelyn Green and Walter Hooper, *C. S. Lewis: A Biography,* rev. ed. (London: HarperCollins, 2002), p. 310.

Chapter 1. The Island

Page 29   "Novelist E. M. Forster was of the opinion": E. M. Forster, *Aspects of the Novel* (1927; reprint, Harmondsworth, U.K.: Penguin, 1971), p. 35.

Page 32   "The total lack of atmosphere repels me": C. S. Lewis, "On Stories," in *On Stories and Other Essays on Literature,* ed. Walter Hooper (New York: Harcourt Brace Jovanovich, 1982), p. 7.

Chapter 2. The Ancient Treasure House

Page 36   "In a letter to a Belfast friend" ("The Name Cair Paravel" box): C. S. Lewis, letter to Arthur Greeves, October 18, 1919, in *They Stand Together: The Letters of C. S. Lewis to Arthur Greeves (1914–1963),* ed. Walter Hooper (London: Collins, 1979), p. 263.

Page 36   "As for the second part of the castle's name" ("The Name Cair Paravel" box): Martha Sammons, *A Guide Through Narnia* (Vancouver, B.C.: Regent College Publishing, 2004), p. 192.

Page 36   "Paul Ford in his *Companion to Narnia*" ("The Name Cair Paravel" box): Paul Ford, *A Companion to Narnia* (San Francisco: HarperSanFrancisco, 2005), p. 126.

Chapter 3. The Dwarf

Page 39   "Most important of all is the structure": Aristotle, *The Poetics,* in *Criticism: The Major Statements,* ed. Charles Kaplan (New York: St. Martin's, 1975), p. 28.

Chapter 4. The Dwarf Tells of Prince Caspian

Page 43   "In an unfinished narrative poem" ("The Name Caspian" box): Warren H. Lewis, ed., *Memoirs of the Lewis Family: 1850–1930* (unpublished manuscript held at the Marion E. Wade Center, 1933), 8:164.

Chapter 5. Caspian's Adventure in the Mountains

Page 47   "C. S. Lewis told me" ("Pauline Baynes" box): Quoted in Walter Hooper, *Past Watchful Dragons* (London: Collins, 1980), p. 83.

Page 47   "Though Pauline Baynes consulted with Lewis" ("Pauline Baynes" box): Quoted in ibid., p. 84.

Page 48   "Spring is . . . not really less beautiful": J. R. R. Tolkien, "On Fairy-

Stories," in *Essays Presented to Charles Williams*, ed. C. S. Lewis (Grand Rapids: Eerdmans, 1966), p. 73.

Chapter 6. The People That Lived in Hiding

Page 51   Roger Lancelyn Green and Walter Hooper, *C. S. Lewis: A Biography*, rev. ed. (London: HarperCollins, 2002), p. 306.

Chapter 8. How They Left the Island

Page 59   "The humanists could not really bring themselves": C. S. Lewis, *English Literature in the Sixteenth Century, Excluding Drama* (Oxford: Oxford University Press, 1954), p. 28.

Page 59   "[In the Narnia stories] we always know" (box): Margaret Patterson Hannay, *C. S. Lewis* (New York: Frederick Ungar, 1981), p. 71.

Chapter 9. What Lucy Saw

Page 62   "[Lewis] was a superb stylist" (box): Rolland Hein, *Christian Mythmakers* (Chicago: Cornerstone, 1998), p. 245.

Page 62   "What a person sees depends on": Peter J. Schakel, *The Way into Narnia: A Reader's Guide* (Grand Rapids: Eerdmans, 2005), p. 56.

Chapter 10. The Return of the Lion

Page 64   "It was in fairy-stories": J. R. R. Tolkien, "On Fairy-Stories," in *Essays Presented to Charles Williams*, ed. C. S. Lewis (Grand Rapids: Eerdmans, 1966), p. 75.

Page 65   "It demands of us a child's love of marvels": C. S. Lewis, *Studies in Medieval and Renaissance Literature*, ed. Walter Hooper (Cambridge: Cambridge University Press, 1966), pp. 132-33.

Page 65   "Peter Schakel suggests": Peter J. Schakel, *The Way into Narnia: A Reader's Guide* (Grand Rapids: Eerdmans, 2005), p. 55.

Page 66   "I found the name in the notes" (box): C. S. Lewis, letter to Carol, January 22, 1952, in *Letters to Children*, ed. Lyle W. Dorsett and Marjorie Lamp Mead (New York: Macmillan, 1985), p. 29.

Chapter 11. The Lion Roars

Page 70   "Our forebears of long ago": Gilbert Murray, *The Classical Tradition in Poetry* (New York: Vintage, 1957), p. 10.

Page 70   "Lewis believed fairy tales" (box): David Colbert, *The Magical Worlds of Narnia* (New York: Berkley, 2005), pp. 1-2.

Chapter 13. The High King in Command

Page 75   "My idea was that the map" ("The Map for *Prince Caspian*" box): C. S. Lewis, letter to Pauline Baynes, January 8, 1951, in *Collected Letters,* ed. Walter Hooper (London: HarperCollins, 2004-2006), 3:83-84.

Chapter 14. How All Were Very Busy

Page 77   "The word *Tellus* comes from the Latin" (box): Walter Hooper, *C. S. Lewis: A Companion and Guide* (San Francisco: HarperSanFrancisco, 1996), p. 414.

Page 78   "Spenser, like all the Elizabethan poets" ("For Reflection or Discussion" box): C. S. Lewis, annotation to a passage from Book 1 of Spenser's *Faerie Queene,* quoted in *Major British Writers,* ed. G. G. Harrison (New York: Harcourt Brace & World, 1959), 1:120.

Chapter 15. Aslan Makes a Door in the Air

Page 81   "In August 1907, after a visit to the London zoo" ("A Fascination with Mice" box): Quoted in Warren H. Lewis, ed., *Memoirs of the Lewis Family: 1850–1930* (unpublished manuscript held at the Marion E. Wade Center, 1933), 3:80.

Page 81   "I love real mice" ("A Fascination with Mice" box): C. S. Lewis, letter to Hila, June 3, 1953, in *Letters to Children,* ed. Lyle W. Dorsett and Marjorie Lamp Mead (New York: Macmillan, 1985), p. 32.

Chapter 16. Are the Narnian Stories Allegorical?

Page 94   "Some people seem to think": C. S. Lewis, "Sometimes Fairy Stories May Say Best What's to Be Said," in *On Stories and Other Essays on Literature,* ed. Walter Hooper (New York: Harcourt Brace Jovanovich, 1982), p. 46.

Page 94   "You are mistaken when you think": C. S. Lewis, letter to American Fifth Grade Class, May 29, 1954, in *Letters to Children,* ed. Lyle W. Dorsett and Marjorie Lamp Mead (New York: Macmillan, 1985), pp. 44-45.

Page 95   "In a certain sense" (box): C. S. Lewis, "On Three Ways of Writing for Children," in *On Stories and Other Essays on Literature,* ed. Walter

Hooper (New York: Harcourt Brace Jovanovich, 1982), p. 41.

Page 95   "By an allegory I mean a composition": C. S. Lewis, letter to Mrs.
           Hook, December 29, 1958, in *Collected Letters,* ed. Walter Hooper
           (London: HarperCollins, 2004-2006), 3:1004.

Page 95   "In reality however [Aslan] is an invention": Ibid., 3:1004-5.

Page 96   "The Narnian series is not exactly allegory": Lewis, letter to Francis
           Anderson, September 23, 1963, in ibid., 3:1460.

Page 97   "In an essay on Bunyan's *Pilgrim's Progress*": C. S. Lewis, *Selected Liter-
           ary Essays* (Cambridge: Cambridge University Press, 1969), p. 149.

Page 97   "That is a flawed way of reading": Ibid.

Page 97   "Of course one does not *need* to read allegory": Ibid.

Page 98   "Let the pictures tell you": Lewis, "On Three Ways of Writing for Chil-
           dren," in *On Stories,* p. 41.

Page 98   "My view would be that a good myth" (box): Letter to Father Peter
           Milward, September 22, 1956, in *Collected Letters,* 3:789-90.

Page 98   "As we know, almost anything": C. S. Lewis, *Reflections on the Psalms*
           (London: Geoffrey Bles, 1958), p. 100.

Page 99   "Lewis's helpful comments": See C. S. Lewis, *An Experiment in Criticism*
           (Cambridge: Cambridge University Press, 1961), pp. 14-26.

Page 99   "The figure of Aslan": Dom Bede Griffiths, *Canadian CSL Journal,* no.
           47, summer 1984, p. 2.

Page 100   "I think that you will probably see": Lewis, letter to Anne Jenkins,
           March 5, 1961, in *Collected Letters,* 3:1244.

Page 100   "Lewis wrote elsewhere": C. S. Lewis, "Sometimes Fairy Stories May
           Say Best What's to Be Said," in *On Stories,* p. 46.

Page 100   "One of Lewis's most provocative statements": C. S Lewis, *The Allegory
           of Love: A Study in Medieval Tradition* (New York: Oxford University
           Press, 1936), p. 60.

Page 101   "Instead of viewing works of literature": Northrop Frye, *Anatomy of
           Criticism* (Princeton, N.J.: Princeton University Press, 1957), pp.
           89-91.

Page 101   "Next we have texts": Ibid., p. 91.

Page 101   "A Spenser scholar named Graham Hough": Graham Hough, *A Preface
           to the Faerie Queene* (New York: W. W. Norton, 1962), pp. 105-11.

Page 102   "Thus Hough claims": Ibid., p. 105.

Page 102   "In the same vein Frye claimed": Frye, *Anatomy of Criticism,* p. 89.

Page 103   "The whole Narnian story" (box): C. S. Lewis, letter to Anne Waller

Jenkins, March 5, 1961, in *Collected Letters,* 3:1244-45.

Page 102 "Lewis himself, in his commentary on Spenser's allegorical technique": See C. S. Lewis, *English Literature in the Sixteenth Century, Excluding Drama* (Oxford: Oxford University Press, 1954), p. 381; and Lewis, *Allegory of Love,* p. 334.

Chapter 17. The Christian Vision of *Prince Caspian*

Page 106 "The whole Narnian story": C. S. Lewis, letter to Anne Waller Jenkins, March 5, 1961, in *Collected Letters,* ed. Walter Hooper (London: HarperCollins, 2004-2006), 3:1244.

Page 107 "Indeed, as Lewis explains elsewhere": Letter to Sophia Storr, December 24, 1959, in ibid., 3:1113.

Page 107 "Writing to answer the questions": Letter to Anne Waller Jenkins, in ibid., 3:1244.

Page 108 "The ethics of fantasy": G. K. Chesterton, *Orthodoxy* (Garden City, N.Y.: Image, 1959), p. 49.

Page 109 "This Rule of Right and Wrong" (box): C. S. Lewis, *Mere Christianity* (New York: Macmillan, 1952), p. 16.

Page 110 "There is no neutral ground" (box): C. S. Lewis, "Christianity and Culture," in *Christian Reflections* (Grand Rapids: Eerdmans, 1967), p. 33.

Page 113 "Or as Schakel explains": Peter J. Schakel, *The Way into Narnia: A Reader's Guide* (Grand Rapids: Eerdmans, 2005), p. 55.

Page 113 "For I do not seek to understand": Anselm, "Proslogian," in *Anselm of Canterbury,* ed. and trans. Jasper Hopkins and Herbert W. Richardson (New York: Edwin Mellon, 1975), 1:93.

Page 113 "[In life] . . . as in the New Testament" (box): C. S. Lewis, "Religion: Reality or Substitute?" in *Christian Reflections* (Grand Rapids: Eerdmans, 1967), p. 43.

Page 114 "There must perhaps always be" (box): Quoted in Sheldon Vanauken, *Encounter with Light* (Wheaton, Ill.: Wade Center, 1979), p. 25.

Page 115 "Elsewhere Lewis comments on how": C. S. Lewis, *Letters to Malcolm* (London: Geoffrey Bles, 1964), p. 109.

Page 116 "We might think that God wanted" (box): Lewis, *Mere Christianity,* p. 63.

Page 116 "At first I had very little idea": C. S. Lewis, "It All Began with a Picture," in *On Stories and Other Essays on Literature,* ed. Walter Hooper (New York: Harcourt Brace Jovanovich, 1982), p. 53.

Page 117 "To love and admire anything" (box): Lewis, *Mere Christianity,* p. 98.

Page 118   "Why is God landing" (box): Ibid., p. 50.

Chapter 18. Contemporary Reviews of *Prince Caspian*

Page 120   "Lewis biographer George Sayer has noted": George Sayer, *Jack: A Life of C. S. Lewis* (Wheaton, Ill.: Crossway, 1994), p. 315.

Chapter 20. A Brief Biography of C. S. Lewis

Page 134   "[C. S. Lewis] aroused warm affection" (box): Helen Gardner, *Clive Staples Lewis: 1898–1963* (London: Oxford University Press, n.d.), p. 418. (Offprint from the Proceedings of the British Academy 51 [1965]: 417-28.)

Appendix A. *The Lion, the Witch and the Wardrobe:* The Movie

Page 138   "On Television last night": Warren H. Lewis, *Brothers and Friends: The Diaries of Major Warren Hamilton Lewis,* ed. Clyde S. Kilby and Marjorie Lamp Mead (San Francisco: Harper & Row, 1982), p. 276.

Appendix B. Using This Guide with Reading Groups

Page 156   "As C. S. Lewis himself advised": C. S. Lewis, *An Experiment in Criticism* (Cambridge: Cambridge University Press, 1961), pp. 19, 134.

Acknowledgments and Permissions

ACKNOWLEDGMENTS

As always, we are grateful to our colleagues at the Marion E. Wade Center, Wheaton College, for the encouragement and support they have offered as we worked on this volume: Director Christopher Mitchell, Heidi Truty, Laura Schmidt and Shawn Mrakovich. In addition we are especially indebted to our Wade research assistant, Rachel Mink, for her able assistance in tracking down various materials, checking citations, preparing the illustration comparison chart and countless other matters. Tony Dawson also deserves our gratitude for his careful reading of the book in manuscript.

Finally we would like to thank the editorial, production and marketing staff of InterVarsity Press for their thorough and skilled work. In particular we are grateful to our editor, Cynthia Bunch, for her dedicated work on our behalf throughout the editorial process.

Index

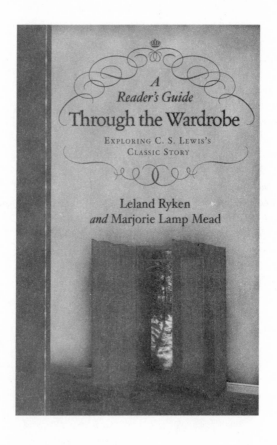